# blur

**The whole story** *by* Martin Roach

OMNIBUS PRESS

London / New York / Paris / Sydney

Exclusive Distributors:
Book Sales Limited
8/9 Frith Street, London W1V 5TZ, UK.
Music Sales Corporation
257 Park Avenue South, New York, NY 10010,
USA.
Music Sales Pty Limited
120 Rothschild Avenue, Rosebery, NSW 2018,
Australia.
To the Music Trade only:
Music Sales Limited
8/9 Frith Street, London W1V 5TZ, UK.

Photo credits:
Front cover: Kevin Cummins/LFI;
All Action: b/c inset, 31b, 35b; Mark Allan/
Alpha: 72, 80, 81, 89, 96; Piers Allardyce/SIN: 30t;
Peter Anderson/SIN: 14, 50; Kelly Ashmore/
Retna: 74r; Colin Bell/Retna: b/c inset;
Dave Bennett/Alpha: 69; Big Pictures: 83t, 88t;
Adrian Callaghan/Retna: 75t; Melanie Cox/
SIN: 19, 38, 39, 41; Andre Csillag/Relay: 75c;
Jeff Davy/Retna: 48; Steve Double/Retna: 36, 53;
Mary Evans Picture Library: 55b, 56c&b;
Simon Exton: 62; Steve Finn/Alpha: b/c inset, 64;
Patrick Ford/Redferns: 82; Patrick Gilbert/SIN: 23;
Steve Gillett: 86; John Gladwin/All Action: 91b;
Martyn Goodacre/SIN: 27, 30b, 31t, 42, 70b, 76,
92, 93; Julian Hawkins: 22; Liane Hentscher/
SIN: 34, 54; Nigel Hildreth: b/c inset, 5, 6, 7, 8, 9,
10, 11, 12; Mick Hutson/Redferns: b/c insets, 24,
43, 45, 49; Alistair Indge/Retna: 40t; Amanda Laine/
Retna: b/c inset, 20, 21; London Features
International: b/c insets, 1, 4, 26, 32, 33, 35t, 37,
40b, 51, 55t, 56t, 57, 59, 60t, 65, 66, 67b, 68L, 71,
73, 74L, 75b, 78b, 79t, 84L, 87t&b, 88b, 90, 91t;
Angela Lubrano: 61t&b; Hayley Madden/SIN: 67t;
Simon Meaker/All Action: 83b; Pappix UK: 70t;
Doug Peters/All Action: 78t, 79b; Andy Roshay:
2, 63; Ed Sirrs/Retna: 60b, 77, 84r, 85;
Nick Tansley/All Action: 29; Kim Tonelli/SIN: 58;
Midori Tsukagoshi/Retna: 52, 68r; Andy Willsher/
SIN: b/c inset, 46, 47.

Every effort has been made to trace the
copyright holders of the photographs in this
book but one or two were unreachable.
We would be grateful if the photographers
concerned would contact us.

Printed in Singapore.

A catalogue record for this book is available
from the British Library.

Acknowledgements:
Many people have been instrumental in
completing this book and my gratitude is
warmly extended to Eddie Deedigan,
Nigel Hildreth, Lucy Stimson, Pat Gilbert,
Philip Glassborow, Biffo, Rets, Ric Blaxill,
Top of the Pops, Chris Twomey, Wiz,
Chris Charlesworth, Hilary Donlon,
Andrew King, Paul Mortlock, Nikki Russell,
Brendan Coyle, Karen Johnson at EMI,
Ellie at Food Records, Ben 'The Youth' Welch,
Krystal 'Kiki' Welch, Andy Linehan and
the National Sound Archive, Paul Aston,
Dave Crook, Paddy at Badmoon,
Roselle Le Sauteur and Steve Wright of

# 1

## All That You Can Do Is Watch Them Play

"No single person here can change the philosophy of this college."

The sentence rang out over the large class of first year drama students. Towards the back of the room, 18-year-old Damon Albarn glanced across at his friend Eddie Deedigan and raised a sceptical eyebrow. After all, this was East 15, a notorious champion of the method acting school of drama, supposedly a cauldron of latent talent and artistic potential.

In recent weeks student dissent and absenteeism had risen in protest at the increasingly strict courses and under-funding. Damon and Eddie had just refused to go to tap dancing, convinced it was not how they wanted to progress. Matters had come to a head and the director was strolling back and forth in front of the class, warning of the grave consequences for any student who didn't toe the line.

She repeated her opening statement. As she did, Damon leant across to Eddie and whispered: "No single person here can change the philosophy of this college eh? – what if that single person is right?"

● ● ●

Damon's Bohemian upbringing had influenced him in a multitude of ways, but the greatest legacy he'd inherited from his parents was unshakeable confidence in his own ideas. His father's family came from a long line of Lincolnshire Quakers and Damon's grandfather had served time during World War Two for being a conscientious objector. Paradoxically, his mother's parents were farmers who accommodated prisoners of war to work on their land during the conflict. Keith Albarn and his bride Hazel married despite their different backgrounds, and soon gave birth to Jessica, followed three years later by Damon, on March 23, 1968, in Whitechapel Hospital. Outside in the big wide world of pop, the swinging Sixties were in full effect and The Beatles had just scooped four Grammy Awards for their latest album 'Sgt. Pepper's Lonely Hearts Club Band'.

Damon at the back of the class and distracted, Residential Orchestral Course, Wicken House, Essex, 1982

It was a great time to be young in London, and the Albarns were deeply involved in the cultural changes that flower power brought. Damon's mother was an accomplished stage designer at the revolutionary Theatre Royal Stratford East company of Joan Littlewood. She worked on many productions, including one, *Mrs Wilson's Diary,* whilst pregnant with Damon. She later went on to have several collections of her art exhibited, and even fashioned the glass bead necklace which Damon wears around his neck to this day.

Damon's father was also involved in the arts. Having trained as an artist, he was the first person to show a Yoko Ono art exhibition in London in 1966 – clearly his mind had to be open to work with Yoko, whom lest we forget was a highly acclaimed and controversial conceptual artist of ten years' standing in her own right before she met her future Beatle husband. Keith Albarn was more than happy to work in an environment where Yoko would ask people to "communicate with the other members by mental telepathy".

Keith later presented a BBC2 arts show with some aplomb which became the pilot production for the *South Bank Show.* He also ran a shop in Kingly Street, just down the road from BBC Broadcasting House, in the heart of psychedelic London. The store was crammed with weird and wonderful furniture, decorations and other design creations of the flowering hippie culture. Like his wife, he enjoyed a keen interest in stage design which was put to good use in his role as manager of Sixties jazz rock warlords Soft Machine. Founded in the year England lifted the World Cup, Soft Machine's early art rock soon evolved through various personnel changes into a fine jazz rock fusion which for many is still the standard against which future forays in this field must be measured. Robert Wyatt, the mercurial singer who left in 1970, provided perhaps the band's highlight with 'Moon In June' which mixed his distinctive humour with a half-spoken, half-sung vocal, delivered in his very English accent.

The band was a progressive theatrical outfit and Keith was heavily involved as their residential concept stage designer. The most famous of Soft Machine's various Dadaist 'happenings' was The Discotheque Interplay in Saint Aygulf, in 1967's summer of love, which achieved much notoriety after the local mayor banned it for making his coastline "look like a pig-sty".

Back in the family home in Leytonstone, east London, the Albarn's immersion in the psychedelic Sixties was fully visible when Damon arrived a year later. Outwardly a small Victorian terraced house, Chez Albarn was hardly *Terry and June.* The lounge was painted silver and all the rooms were furnished with bizarre conceptual pieces that his father sold in his shop. In amongst the clutter were presents from the various artists and performers who would visit, including some odd blue chairs that were once the property of Cat Stevens.

From an early age, Damon and his sister were treated as young adults rather than small children and they were both always welcome at the many parties held at the house. On these occasions, the home would be filled with strange characters, musicians, artists and performers. As befitting

the period, drugs were inevitably present, but the Albarns kept them strictly clear of the children and avoided hard drug use themselves. They did occasionally shelter hard drug addicts, but their admirable attitude with the children never wavered.

Years later at a Blur gig, journalists were surprised to see Damon smoking a joint while talking to his father. For Damon, this was never an issue, as he told *Q* magazine: "Pop culture was never something new to me. It never served as a reference point for rebellion. I was always allowed to stay up late around at parties with people smoking dope and getting pissed and taking drugs." Damon also said "I had a very open childhood, in many ways, which didn't hold me back or fill me with masses of angst."

Damon's first ten years were spent in this liberal atmosphere, and his impressionable mind greedily absorbed the colourful environment. Attending the George Thompson Primary School in Leytonstone, Damon was a perfectly normal, ordinary young child. He played football, occasionally listened to music, collected stuffed animals and fossils, enjoyed bird watching and avoided girls. At seven he went to his first musical, *The Point* at the Camden Roundhouse, which was a similar production to the hugely successful *Hair*. Damon's other key memory of his primary years was watching the silent monks from a nearby monastery taking their morning walks through the woods near his home. Such a progressive upbringing inevitably influences a child, and Damon is quite sure it fuelled his later lyrical obsession with the mundane, as he told *The Face* "Normal life is fascinating. That's where I want to be. I started my life in a fucking hippie forest with monks and chrysanthemums."

Damon's first real upheaval came in his tenth year. He was taken on holiday to Turkey with some friends of the family for two months and when he returned his parents had moved to Colchester. His father had landed an excellent job running the local art college, and the Albarns had moved into a comfortable four bedroom 14th century house. It was a prestigious position and Keith Albarn strengthened his reputation by writing two books on Islamic design, including *The Language Of Patterns*. For Albarn Junior, however, the change was not so immediately beneficial. Having been more than comfortable in the multi-racial, liberal atmosphere of London, where his family's colourful ways were easily accepted, Damon now found himself in Small Town England with stifling values and morals.

Damon began attending Stanway Comprehensive School, and during his first year found that his extrovert character was generally unwelcome. Any new boy at school is always at a disadvantage, and although he wasn't bullied, Damon's home life and expansive interests made him something of a 'weirdo' or, even worse, the ultimate sin, a 'gay boy'. By now, Damon had begun learning the violin, and was reading the works of Karl Marx; he loved drama, listened to music and sported an ear-ring, none of which were likely to earn him much respect with tough, football playing, hard drinking, women-chasing 12-year-old hell raisers. Conversely, Damon's pretty features and extrovert nature attracted certain pupils him, especially those with a similar interest in the arts

Opposite: Top of the class, Colchester
Sixth Form College, December 1994

Shortly after Damon arrived at Stanway, the school appointed a new Head of Music, Nigel Hildreth, who brought with him an open attitude to the subject that Damon has since publicly recognised as vital to his development. Hildreth enjoyed a love/hate relationship with the young Albarn throughout Damon's time at Stanway, recognising and encouraging his talent but being frustrated by Damon's frequent lapses.

"What is most noticeable from this period is that Damon's music was very much secondary to his fervent interest in drama and an acting career," says Hildreth. "I recall his mother telling me that 'Damon's talents are not in music' and he felt the same. Damon felt his skills were in acting rather than music and he was always heavily involved in our school productions. He made his stage début in a show called *Fist*, which was a rock opera adaptation I had written of the Faust legend. As a third year, Damon was only in the chorus, but he was still very much into it.

Damon as Bobby 'The Boyfriend'

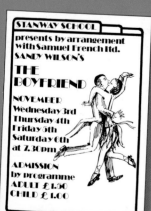

"After that, we did a whole range of pieces in which Damon was always involved, with increasingly important roles. His enthusiasm was such that even if he was not on stage he would find his way backstage to be part of the crew. He played his first lead as Bobby in *The Boyfriend*, a 1920s musical by Andy Wilson, where he had to dance the Charleston. He also went on to play Nathan Detroit in *Guys and Dolls*, and Jupiter, King of the Gods in *Orpheus In The Underworld*, which was his final performance. Interestingly, this particular part showed that although his acting talent was not in question, his singing was not technically up to operetta."

This production also showed the extent of Damon's confidence – at one point the weapon with which he was

supposed to be attacking someone fell apart, but he saved the show from disaster by calmly ad-libbing the whole of the next scene.

For Damon, the performance was everything. This practical approach soon affected his 'O' level music studies, where he found difficulty applying himself to the theory based course. Even on the preferred playing side, his school instrument, the violin, was soon superseded by his growing interest in the piano. Hildreth saw his talent grow but no more than most competent pupils.

"He was quite an accomplished improviser on the piano, although about normal for a good student. It was *never* a case of 'a star is born'," says Hildreth. "To be honest, he had some problems when playing from written music, with timing, with his rhythm. Nevertheless, he played second violin regularly with The Colne Valley Youth Orchestra and with our own Stanway Orchestra, but was frequently chastised for not concentrating. This was particularly frustrating, because when it came to his own music he had no such problems. He took some jazz piano classes of his own volition with a local blind teacher called Rich Webb, and was always encouraged in his artistic endeavours by both his parents, who had an excellent attitude. Having said that, it is very difficult to see any outstanding glimmers at that stage, certainly not in his music – his compositions were good, but nothing outstanding. Where I saw the best of his work was definitely in his acting performance – his stage presence and ability were very definite. He had a tangible magnetism on stage and many of the teachers thought he could make it as an actor."

Gradually Damon's compositions did develop. "He was always into composition as well. He developed this ability to extemporise and take from all areas of music, a trait which I feel has always been Blur's major strength. Through a mixture of my encouragement and his own volition, he gained a basic understanding of musicals, classical, jazz, rock, orchestral and many other forms. You could see in his own compositions that he was using all of these reference points."

Away from classes, Damon loved his keyboard but rarely played his violin. The classical proclivity of his course work introduced him to many great writers, of whom Vaughan Williams was a particular favourite. To complement this, his parents' assorted record collection opened his young ears to music that was unusually diverse for his age. Soft Machine were an obvious feature, but Kurt Weill, various jazz masters and even Rod Stewart were regular visitors to the Albarn turntable. At the opposite extreme, Damon spent six months in front of his bedroom mirror pretending to be the dandy highwayman Adam Ant. But it was the rise of 2-Tone that had the biggest effect on Damon's music and it was through the short-lived black and white chequered ska boom that he first met Graham Coxon.

The biggest selling independent single of 1979 was 'Gangsters' by The Specials, released on their own 2-Tone record label, and this heralded a genuine chart invasion of similar 2-Tone bands whose music was a curious mixture of modern styles drawing heavily on Jamaican ska.

Technically proficient covers of Prince Buster, The Pioneers, The Skatalites and The Maytals were complemented by 2-Tone's own intelligent compositions, perhaps most notably when The Specials 'Too Much Too Young' topped the UK charts. Madness, The Beat and Selector were the best known bands but there was more to the scene than just music. "The clothes are almost as important," Specials leader Terry Hall told *NME*. "We're not a mod band or a skinhead band, the rude boy thing is a real mixture."

Having the right trousers, the correct shoes and just the right size pork pie hat was crucial to being a cool rude boy. Graham Coxon's brogues were cheap imitations, but most pupils let this pass. However, there is always one bastard at school who picks up on your minor fashion *faux pas*, and in this instance it was Damon Albarn. Despite hardly knowing Graham, Damon walked over to him during a school trip and publicly ridiculed his cheap footwear. Damon, of course, had the genuine article.

Despite this odd start, the two found they had similar tastes in many things, particularly music, and very soon a close friendship developed. Both boys covered their school books in monochrome 2-Tone logos, with Madness and The Specials taking pride of place. Graham's saxophone, drum, and basic guitar playing matched Damon's own musical aptitude and soon they were swapping records and going to youth clubs together in full Nutty Boy regalia. Although most of their female peers were into soul, the two friends were unimpressed. Damon still applauds these bands and cites 2-Tone as a major influence on the material he would later write: "Madness are immensely important folk heroes in British pop music."

At this stage Graham's greatest gift was his art – his drawing and paintings (which began with him copying Beatles record sleeves) were stunning. He and Damon seemed very alike, but they came from very different backgrounds. Graham's father Bob was in the RAF, and it was during one of many postings abroad that Graham was born, in a military hospital in Rinteln, in Germany, four years after his sister Hayley. Coxon Senior was a bandsman, a commendable clarinettist and saxophonist, so the household was musical, with Beatles records playing constantly.

Graham was given his first instrument, a fife, when he was just six. His infant years were spent on an RAF estate in Berlin, and at five he moved to live with his grandfather next to a flyover in Derby. Like Damon, his tenth year brought upheaval. His father left the RAF and became a conductor for the Essex Constabulary Police Band, moving the family home to Colchester in the process. Bob Coxon also became a visiting music teacher at Stanway, and sent his own son to the school.

Damon was a school year older then Graham but that made no difference to their friendship. The Coxon house ran on to the back of the school playing fields and during lunch times the pair would head for Graham's tiny bedroom

which housed a cheap drum kit , and listen to music, surrounded by posters of The Jam on every wall. A Jam B-side 'Aunties & Uncles' was the first song Graham learned to play on his guitar. At other times, they would stay in the music block during the break and play through songbooks given to them by Mr Hildreth that included classic material by Simon & Garfunkel and Lennon & McCartney. When they weren't playing music, they would watch Mike Leigh's *Meantime* or *Quadrophenia*, yearning to be Phil Daniels as Jimmy the Mod.

Lucy Stimson, a classmate, recalls Graham's other obsession. "He was always going around school talking about Keith Moon of The Who, it was Moon this and Moon that, on and on. He even had a Who video and watched it all the time. He was so into Moon, and of course this helped his enthusiasm for drumming."

Graham was also studying for 'O' level music, but was markedly less extrovert than Damon, as Hildreth recalls: "Graham was always much quieter. He was always very dedicated and quite serious. Whereas Damon's year was not that talented, Graham found himself amongst a very good group of pupils, which he found a little intimidating at times. He always undervalued his own musical ability, which was a shame because he has a very intuitive sense of musicality, he has a lot of skills and a great feel for the music. I remember quite clearly him playing his first saxophone solo, and he played it very musically indeed."

Both boys' enthusiasm for music began to pay off – they became promising classical musicians, and both had original compositions performed by the Essex Youth Orchestra. One of Damon's works was even good enough to win a regional heat in the *Young Musician Of The Year* competition. Damon's non-classical compositions were often aired at school shows. For *A Summer Extravaganza*, Damon played a piece he had written on his keyboard, with his friend James Hibbins singing.

It wasn't long before Damon and Graham appeared on stage together. Graham was Styx, servant of Pluto,

Essex County Standard, May 10, 1985

The senior band bought the first half of the concert to a rousing close with three pieces Take Five, A Trumpeters Lullaby and Big Band Jazz. Soloist Graham Coxon and Helen Fisher both deserve special praise for their assuredly musical play.

Damon Albarn (piano) and Graham Coxon (saxophone) performed one of his compositions from a Basement Window. This was particularly well received and it is worth mentioning that Mr Albarn was the only performer to acknowledge his applause by taking a bow.

Right: Damon and his
'Amazing Technicolour' make-up

in *Orpheus In The Underworld* while Damon was Jupiter, and he had a minor role in *Oh, What A Lovely War*, again with Damon. Another time, when the school put on *The Bartered Bride* in collaboration with The Royal Opera House, Graham was in the chorus with Damon's sister Jessica, and they both appeared in full make-up on a televised performance for *Blue Peter*. Graham was acutely embarrassed as he had to wear his trousers tucked into his socks all day, but he earned his *Blue Peter* badge nonetheless. Damon was too busy taking his 'O' level exams and had to make do with helping out backstage.

On a few occasions they actually played in the same band at school. The first was an ad-hoc group assembled for a school show in which Damon (keyboards) and Graham (saxophone) were joined by their friends Paul Stevens (guitar), James Hibbins (guitar and vocals), Michael Morris (guitar) and Kevin Ling (drums). They performed two songs that Damon had written, the titles of which have been lost to posterity amongst the fairy cakes and tombola prizes. Hildreth clearly remembers the flowering of Damon's stagecraft. "Damon could attract an audience and communicate in such a way that they were literally left screaming for more," he says.

Soon Damon and Graham formed their first band outside of school. Damon was as influenced by recent pop events as anyone else: "The Smiths were the best band in the world, we all wanted to dress like Morrissey, give up meat like Morrissey." He also claims that The Smiths' singer spurred him on to forming bands himself: "What made me be in a band was seeing a *South Bank Show* on The Smiths and hearing Morrissey say that pop music was dead, and that The Smiths had been the last group of any significance. I remember thinking 'No-one is going to tell me that pop music is finished'."

The first real outfit of any note was The Aftermath, which contained Damon, Graham, James Hibbins and another school friend Paul Stevens. Their only real moment of fame was playing the Jimi Hendrix Experience arrangement of 'Hey Joe' to school assembly. After that, Hibbins left and was replaced by Alistair Havers, and the new band was christened Real Lives . All the time, Damon was writing – one of his first pop songs was about a diamond run from Amsterdam to Johannesburg, inspired by a TV documentary he had seen.

As Damon's extra-curricular activities drew him increasingly away from his course work, he often came into conflict with Nigel Hildreth. "He could be extremely exasperating, because people knew he had it in him but he had his own agenda," he says. "More often than not, he would be in a world of his own, even during productions and shows. He would regularly not be on stage when he should have been, missing lines or cues, the inevitable slip up. He would be most apologetic, and take the criticism, he realised he was out of line, but he just couldn't help himself and would still do it again.

"There were times when I really lost my rag with him, he could be a real loose cannon. Interestingly, his fellow students seemed not to mind, they knew he was like that. Also, when he did concentrate, he could deliver the goods."

Lucy Stimson recalls that Damon's lack of commitment

was noticed by everyone. "At the time he took his 'O' levels he wasn't famous for his classical music. There was a cruel joke going around about Damon that in the 'O' level paper, the first question was 'How many strings does a violin have?' The joke was that Damon put six."

Damon passed his 'O' levels (including music) and decided to stay on at Stanway, studying music, English and history in the sixth form. The 'A' level music was considerably harder than anything he'd attempted before.

"He enjoyed various elements of the course, such as the history and the composition, but he struggled elsewhere," says Nigel Hildreth. "He must have enjoyed it to a degree, and he was always incredibly well-meaning. He was always very keen on the music, working on it he contributed a lot, and worked well with the other students. However, by now you could see he had his own agenda."

Damon's group Real Lives had by now established themselves as a going concern and performed several gigs, including one at The Affair club in Colchester. Their most noted performance was actually at the school. Some sixth formers had to create a limited company for a business project and Graham's class mate Lucy Stimson had the idea that they should put on a live gig for the first and second years.

"It was just something different from their normal disco," she recalls. "Real Lives played all original material and the kids went absolutely mad for it, they were a smash hit. Damon in particular had this magnetism on stage. As a fellow pupil, it was absolutely abundantly clear that he was far from ordinary. His presence simply wasn't normal and the teachers and the pupils knew it. He never excelled at classical, but on stage he had that something extra, without a doubt. There are very few people who stand out at Secondary school age, but Damon did easily."

Away from school work and bands, Graham and Damon went on a summer holiday to Romania with Graham's parents. The remainder of their education was spent snogging their first girlfriends, buying as many records as they could afford and getting drunk on cheap wine and smoking bad cigars.

Lucy Stimson remembers that Damon was always more successful with girls than his friend. "Damon was very charming and with his acting ability he was very popular, although not really until the sixth form. Lots of girls liked him. Graham meanwhile was much more shy and reserved, but he was always a very sweet character. He did seem to struggle with girls more than Damon because of that quieter nature. Neither of them were yobs, there were no real dirty stories or shady episodes. They were seen by fellow pupils as friendly and sweet."

The inevitable result of these distractions was that Damon failed his 'A' level music (as well as his Grade 8 theory). "There were two key factors which led to Damon failing his 'A' level," says Hildreth. "Firstly, he had decided beyond question that he wanted to go to drama school,

STANWAY SCHOOL
*in collaboration with*
THE ROYAL OPERA
*presents*
SMETANA'S
The Bartered Bride

JULY 8 – 11, 1986
at **7.30** p.m.

MERCURY THEATRE
COLCHESTER

**Chorus of villagers, actors, children.**

Jessica Albarn
Karen Banks
Alison Blewett
Stuart Carey
Joanne Carey
Graham Coxon
Helen Fisher
Jocelyn Fuller
Rebecca Gladden
Darren Gooding
Neil Gower
Sarah Honeyball
Andrew Humm
Justin Lunniss
Alistair MacDonald
Neil MacDonald
Julie Pybus
Jackie Rhodes
Faye Rhodes
Paul Stevens
Clare Tenner
Kate Wackett
Simon Williams

Guys and Dolls: Damon Centre Stage, Graham back row, fifth from right

With Samantha Torrington in Guys and Dolls

and so the discipline needed for the music course simply wasn't there. Secondly, the qualification itself wasn't something he was that keen on – when you really got down to the nitty gritty of 'A' level music, where he was required to sit a three hour silent harmony exam, he just wasn't interested. He even brought the wrong music scores for one performance exam.

"There was a conflict between us as a result, because I felt he could have achieved the grade if he had tried. He had the potential but he was not using all of his talents. In retrospect, I don't hold that against him because to a certain extent he had taken what he wanted from the course – the exam was just unnecessary icing on the cake to him. By taking the course, he had learnt several things – his playing was fine, he had some starting points of composition, he knew about basic harmonies, and had

acquired a broad listening base of musical knowledge. That was what the course offered and he took that, the final exam was irrelevant."

Having said that, Damon was sufficiently worried about his poor results (he got an E and D in History and English respectively), that he lied to his parents about them.

Lucy Stimson confirms that Damon was frequently distracted from the course work. "If he wasn't interested in something then he just wouldn't apply himself. That is purely and simply the sign of someone with creative talent who wants to spend time working on those skills. My over-riding memory of Damon at school was him crouched over the piano in the music room, completely oblivious to everyone around him, writing and improvising his own music. Sometimes Graham and the other band members would join in, but quite frequently he was on his own."

Graham had also started 'A' level music in the lower sixth, but he struggled more than Damon with the staid theoretical bias of the course. Halfway through the first year, he gave up. Instead, he headed for The North Essex School Of Art to begin a two year foundation course in General Art and Design, temporarily breaking up the friendship. One connection remained however: the college was run by Damon's father.

Meanwhile, Damon had already auditioned and been accepted at the infamous East 15 drama school in East London. So by their late teens, both Damon and Graham were actively pursuing interests outside of music. Damon went to tell Mr Hildreth about his decision, and explained that drama was his first love, as his teacher had suspected. Mr Hildreth suggested that quite often the music comes back to people, but Damon was adamant: "The music means nothing to me, I am really into the drama."

CERBERUS ENTERPRISES presents:

# REAL LIVES

## IN CONCERT

### at STANWAY SCHOOL

G COXON

**MONDAY APRIL 21st**

**7/10 pm**

Drums,
Saxophone:  Graham Coxon, is responsible for the 'Moonist' revival movement in England. He has also developed his own unique language, known as 'Keng', which we all speak fluently. Recently he had to take the hard decision of whether or not to give up his promising academic career and persue an artistic one ...he choose the artistic one!
Is he a virtuoso?......he plays drums like a manic fart
Is he a prolific writer?..... avant-garde
Vices?.........booze
Interested in politics?........ask him

*

Vocals,
Piano:  Damon Albarn, unlike the other members in the group, is a complete and utter idiot, who is famous for his hair flick and big mouth. A ladies man to the bone, Damon enjoys the fruits of life and this is reflected in his deep and meaningless lyrics, which he usually forgets anyhow.
Is he a virtuoso?....... 'bottoms'
Is he a prolific writer?........ big bottoms
Vices?......... his mouth
Interested in politics?....... ask him.

**THE BRIEF HISTORY of REAL LIVES**

After a brief period spent on 'jazz-trip' Graham & Damon decided that Hibbins should be expelled from the group (ha!). To replace him they called Paul Stevens, who had recently recovered from an attack of 'feedback' After only a week, they had written and recorded two songs and played their **first gig** (it was at this early venue that they had their first encounter with 'pre-pubescent hysteria' - it was not the last!!). For the next few months, they took time off to get their act together and 'dry up'. In July 1985, Havers 'the lad' joined as 'pseudo-bassist'. Together they wrote some 'truly memorable' songs and in December they played in front of 150 people at Stanway. Since then, Havers 'the lad' has enjoyed the life of a 'rock-star' while the other members have written and played his bass lines.

**TICKETS: £1.30**

# 2

## Try, Try, Try

In September 1986, Damon caught the Central Line tube to Debden, where he was starting the three year course at East 15. The school was a stalwart supporter of method acting whereby students must actually live their roles so as to better understand them. The policy obviously worked, as among its ex-pupils the school boasted Alison Steadman and many of the Mike Leigh group. However, on a practical level, for 18-year-old Damon travelling to work as a high-heeled tart, or returning home to a flat in Leytonstone as Ayatollah Khomeini, this presented not inconsiderable difficulties.

Within a few days of the opening term, Damon had struck up a friendship with a fellow first year called Eddie Deedigan, who was three years his senior. Most drama pupils at the college were older than Damon, who was precociously young to be starting the course. Discovering they were into similar writers and music, they became fast friends.

"If we had group debates with a director, it always used to end up with me and Damon talking," recalls Eddie. "That really interested me, this younger guy talking with great knowledge about all manner of subjects. At that point, his confidence was really striking, he could talk well and always with this great sense of humour."

As with all school friends there was plenty of fooling around, but beneath it all there was an intelligence, tenacity and drive developing in Damon that was very noticeable. Eddie learnt early on that his new friend's knowledge could be most helpful: "We were in this class about the history of music in theatre, and this really boring lecturer was asking a variety of obscure questions about baroque that no-one in the room knew anything about. Except Damon. However, instead of being the class know-all and answering all the questions himself, he started to whisper every answer into my ear, which I then told the lecturer. This guy had previously thought I was a prize working class twat, but here I was coming out with all these amazing answers. Everyone was stunned. Damon and myself pissed ourselves laughing."

The two shared many more laughs together at East 15. One project was to live as roaming gypsies in the 1500s. Most of the class toiled away building historically authentic dwelling tents, and living a sparse and frugal life but Eddie and Damon had different ideas. They decided to be travelling gypsy musicians, christened themselves Marco and Alexandro, and spent five weeks sitting under a blossom tree playing guitar and fiddle. For another project, they were transported 150 years in time to a mid-17th century England gripped by the Black Death. "The college gardens needed re-landscaping, so suddenly we are all supposed to be plague-infested labourers working the land," says Eddie. "Like a total twat I grew a beard and spent six weeks digging, but somehow Damon had managed to get himself cast as the bloody landlord. So he just strolled around with this stupid accent telling us what to do, and we couldn't argue because he was the top man."

Although he was primarily at East 15 to learn drama, many of the assignments involved music, and by now Damon was an exceptionally gifted pupil, particularly on piano. For a project called 'A Night In The Longhorn Saloon' Eddie felt that simply churning out the same old tired Western saloon sequence would be too obvious. Instead, he suggested writing a piece about the plight of the American Indians, but no-one except Damon agreed. As a compromise they agreed to do the saloon scene but with original music.

"Within minutes Damon had penned this superb Western theme tune, and I made up some words which went 'I wanna sing in a Western, walk like big John Wayne, I wanna kill a hundred Injuns, then shoot myself in the brain'. The rest of the class were gobsmacked because it sounded amazing, but they just didn't get it, it was a total piss-take. Later on we wrote a song for a friend and Damon just slipped into this lovely lilting Irish ballad, easy. It was only fun, but it showed that Damon was already completely versatile. Within a few months he was doing operas, and playing piano for the college musicals, reciting Brecht and Weill, all sorts of stuff, no problem." Damon even played with the visiting Berliner Ensemble for a Brecht Festival, a highly prestigious accolade for the youngster.

Although not technically proficient as an actor, Damon was frequently the most watchable during college productions. Sometimes this caused friction. "He shone, not as a great actor, just as an immense personality," says Eddie. "At a drama college that is quite an achievement. He looked good, had a great voice as well as this amazing aura about him. Couple that with him being so young and I think that intimidated a lot of people.

"He even unsettled one of the lecturers, who was actually on a weekly television show himself. He was really quite famous but for some reason he just couldn't handle Damon. One time we were performing *The Duchess of Malfi* and Damon was just pleasing himself, and you could see this lecturer getting really irate. Eventually he cracked and said 'Damon, you think you are a god, and the fact is you probably are, but will you please listen to some direction.' The thing is Damon didn't need direction because he wasn't trying to be an actor, he was just exploring that side of expression.

"A few weeks later we were at a student party and by now this same lecturer was really pissed off with Damon, you could see it in his eyes, he felt really threatened. Damon's confidence is a weird thing, at times it seems almost physically threatening when he looks at you. This lecturer was getting very drunk, and he decided to sort Damon out because he knew it would be put down to the alcohol. So he started having a go at Damon and he got really out of order, saying how much better and more talented he was. Damon just waited for his chance and calmly said 'Is that why your wife left you?' The lecturer flew at him, grabbed him by the throat and pinned him to the wall. All the time Damon was just looking at him in this confident way of his, calm as fuck. That really struck me, being on a national television show every week, and still being that threatened by an 18-year-old."

When he wasn't baiting lecturers, Damon was becoming increasingly prolific in his compositions. Eddie himself was working on a promising musical career, but when he had

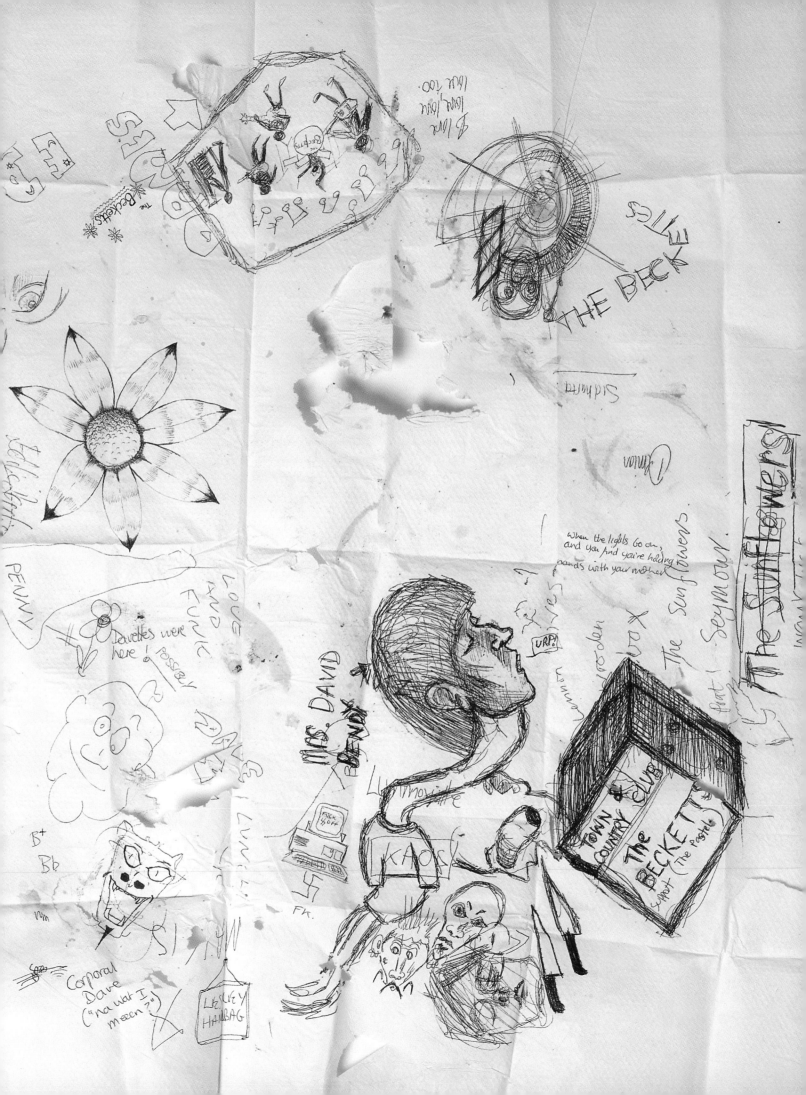

enrolled at East 15 his previous band had split up. Eddie kept the name The Alternative Car Park to fulfil a gig obligation in November of the first term. It was a gig he couldn't afford to miss, a support slot to one of his all-time favourite performers, Nico, formerly of The Velvet Underground, who was on the tail end of a tour to promote her *Camera Obscura* album.

"I had this brilliant actor called Oscar Stringer on saxophone, and a guy called Roy playing just snare. On backing vocals we had this girl called Chris who wore a short skirt and fishnets – she was completely wrong for the set up, not least because her powerful voice nearly blew me offstage. I knew Damon was amazing on keyboards, so I asked if he was interested and he said 'Yeah, no problem, what for?' I casually said 'Oh, you know, we've got this support slot with Nico', and Damon said 'Who's he then?' I said 'Nico, you twat, you know, the fucking Velvet Underground?' and he said 'Who are they then?'"

Eddie played him some Nico and Velvet Underground material, Damon thought it was cool and agreed to play the gig. Unfortunately, because he was in big demand for college musical projects, he had to miss the first three rehearsals. When he finally found some free time, Damon sat and listened to Oscar and Eddie play the songs they had been rehearsing. When they had finished he said "Did you know you're both playing in completely separate keys?" Eddie continues: "He just told Oscar to do this, told me to do that and in five minutes he put us all together. This fucking kid had sorted us all out, and it was my songs!"

The Alternative Car Park with Damon, Eddie and fish-net clad horror, Gold Diggers Chippenham, November 1986

The night of the gig arrived and the band travelled to Gold Diggers in Chippenham, followed by a bus full of their fellow students for moral support. The gig went well, and at the end the rest of the band left the stage so that Damon could play a song of his own which he had been rehearsing with just the fish-net clad singer. He shuffled up to the mike and rather sheepishly apologised in advance: "Sorry, but this is another slow one." Eddie continues the story: "My songs are relatively sad and they were well received. Then Damon came on and did this song of his called 'The Rain' and it just fucking blew us away. There were 300 or 400 people in the audience and they were just amazed, it was a great ballad. That style of song was my vernacular, but 'The Rain' just blew us away." Eddie consoled himself by talking to Nico, who made his decade worthwhile by allowing him to buy her a beer.

Although most of his peers preferred pop, Damon still found huge inspiration in classical music. Much has been made of his fascination with Bertolt Brecht which he said was... "overwhelmingly articulate music. It had more influence on me than any pop record." Brecht wrote contemporary music that was intended to be highly popular, using simple forms and melodies, but with a quirkiness and chromatic nuance that made them unusual. The origins of much of Blur's more unusual material can be traced back to this period. When Damon performed Brecht's *Die Drei Groschen Oper* with the Berliner Ensemble, Damon's old music teacher Nigel Hildreth was in the audience, and afterwards he went out for a curry with his former charge.

"There was a definite progression at that show, he was by now very accomplished, and technically very assured," says Hildreth. "When we ate afterwards the shift in his interests away from drama back towards music was very clear." For his part, Damon thanked Hildreth for shouting at him during school rehearsals and said, "It made me realise that performing was important and it prepared me for the harsh treatment given out at drama school."

After each college day, Damon would return home to the digs he now shared with Eddie and sit in his bedroom writing yet more songs. His hunger for knowledge was reaping rich rewards in the breadth of his material, and Eddie is in no doubt that Damon's parents should take much of the credit for this:.

"His upbringing is crucial, being so open, it gave him all these hundreds of influences. Someone like myself and a lot of contemporary writers, who come from a very working class background haven't been educated in the same way. I went to comprehensive school just as he did, but my upbringing gave me a far narrower scope of reference. I think his parents' lives were extremely influential – he could learn by their example. That shows even now... you can talk to him about certain things, such as music, art and books, but then he's off, and you can't really catch him, he's gone. He seems to know so much more about other things."

Damon agrees, as he told the press: "I always thought my parents were dead right. I was going against the grain in a weird way, by continually following my parents. It just seems to have worked for generations in my family."

Despite the hilarious experiences they shared, both Eddie and Damon soon became disillusioned with East 15. Over-populated classes and under-funded resources fuelled student dissent and absenteeism. Shortly after the "no single person can change this" statement, Eddie and Damon left. Ironically, Damon had gone to East 15 to pursue his childhood ambitions in acting, but it had turned him into a music-obsessed 19-year-old.

Once he had left East 15, Damon's musical focus sharpened. He took various odd jobs to earn money for demos and to buy cheap drink, but was frequently sacked for fooling around. He lost a fruit picking job for doing wheelies in the farm's tractor. He also worked as a barman at The Portobello Hotel, a rock star haunt where he served The Edge and Bono from U2 (all he remembers is that Bono was rude to him). That job didn't last long either and Damon had to rely on shifts at Le Croissant in Euston Station as his main source of income. Fortunately, he had £3,000 inheritance money and this was spent on new gear and a basic demo. This crude tape was then taken to The Beat Studios in Christopher Place in Euston, whose key client was a post-fame Belouis Some.

Owners Maryke Bergkamp and Graeme Holdaway were immediately impressed and agreed to manage Damon and give him free studio time in exchange for a job as a tea boy. This was ideal for Damon, because he could work all day at Le Croissant, then head to The Beat Factory and notch up more studio time. The owners had more preconceived ideas for him – soon after taking the job, he was introduced to a high-pitched singer called Sam, and on the management's urging formed a soul pop duo called Two's A Crowd. The Beat Factory obviously had high hopes for them and a series of industry showcases were quickly arranged. The shows were heavily attended by record company scouts and there were lengthy negotiations over possible contracts. Some sources suggest that Damon sometimes appeared in full stage make-up as a mime artist. Unfortunately, the interest rapidly dried up and the ill-fated group split. This had been Damon's first sniff of possible success, but he wasn't remotely bothered and just carried on writing.

With the demise of Two's A Crowd, Damon formed a band called Circus with a friend Tom Aitkenhead from Chippenham. This music was much more guitar based than Two's A Crowd, but the band's early progress was hampered by the failure to nail down a firm line-up. After several personnel changes, Damon got back in touch with Eddie, who was now living near Clapham Common, and suggested they renew their previous musical partnership. Eddie was reluctant. The Two's A Crowd material did not appeal to him. But Damon played him a demo of the new songs and Eddie loved them, and agreed to join on the spot.

The search for new members continued. Eddie roped in a work mate from Dixons electrical store in Marble Arch called Dave Brolan, who played both bass and guitar. He also recruited Darren Filkins, formerly of The Alternative Car Park (whom Damon had replaced for the Nico support slot), who had just returned from a year travelling around the world, so he took on lead guitar duties. The drummer's slot was also easily filled. Damon knew of a renowned drummer from Colchester with whom he had some loose associations in the past. His name was Dave Rowntree. It was October 1988.

The new Circus line-up began recording the material Damon had written, and for the next two months worked hard in the studio honing their sound, with the aim of recording an album in the New Year. At first everything went well, the songs sounded great, the members gelled and the whole outfit was taking cohesive shape. Then, just two days before they were due to start recording, Darren Filkins announced he had won his first commission as a professional photographer. The band knew he had been hoping for this but didn't expect it to happen quite so suddenly. They were all devastated – except Damon, who shrugged his shoulders and said "That's his choice, I'll phone my friend to do some guitar."

Despite Damon's brave face, the band were hugely deflated. Their songs were well rehearsed, intricate and ready for recording – whoever was brought in at such short notice would only be able to cover over the cracks, and their efforts would be wasted. Damon called his friend anyway, a chap who had done a little saxophone work on some odd meandering instrumentals of his in the past. Two days later, the eleventh hour replacement guitarist walked into the studio, and introduced himself as Graham Coxon.

# 3

## Come Together

Towards the end of his time at Stanway, Graham had become more of an extrovert, something of a common room clown. A school report described him as "a gregarious extrovert who would do well to channel his energies in the future." Those energies were increasingly being directed towards his guitar. Having stopped at Grade Five, his saxophone was no longer his main instrument, and when he moved to The North Essex School Of Art, his guitar playing continued unabated.

Like Damon, he worked various odd jobs, including a two month, twice weekly spell at Sainsburys, as well as a pea-picking job which he later described as "a human combine harvester". He also became a protest vegetarian for a while, but didn't monitor his diet well and ended up with malnutrition in Severals Hospital in Colchester. This was actually the local mental hospital, so Graham spent seven long days cadging fags from senile old men. It also lost him his job at Sainsburys.

Graham then flitted through various bands, including a largely improvisational outfit called The Curious Band. He graduated from the North Essex School Of Art and enrolled on a fine art course at Goldsmiths' College in south east London. Despite leanings towards music, Graham was still a keen artist, and among the students taking the same course was future Turner Prize winner Damien Hirst.

Damon had kept in touch with Graham regularly since they both left school. Graham had also gone along to a solo gig of Damon's at Colchester Arts Centre as moral support, where by coincidence Dave Rowntree was in the crowd. Damon had enrolled at Goldsmiths' as well, on a part time course just to get on campus, so the two friends saw each other often. When Damon asked him to help them out at Beat Factory for the Circus album session, Graham was more than happy. When he turned up at the studio and found Dave on drums, he was even more comfortable – this was not the first time they had played together.

Dave had occasionally called on Graham's services to bolster the brass section in his own band Idle Vice. One of Graham's own loosely formed bands, Hazel Dean And The Carp Enters From Hell, had even played a small local gig called The Anti-Yuppie Festival in Wivenhoe alongside Idle Vice. The connection went even further back than that – when Dave had enrolled at Saturday morning jazz classes as a teenager, he found himself being taught by Bob Coxon, Graham's dad.

Once in the studio with Circus, Graham was shown a couple of songs and they gave it a try. Eddie was stunned. "He fucking licked it, mental playing, unbelievable," he says. "He played this incredible guitar, we were completely blown away by it and then he said 'Is that alright?' Fucking hell, it was alright. We couldn't believe what we were hearing. It was easy for him."

After that, Graham slotted in effortlessly, and the band managed to record the entire album live in just four days. The tracks were highly melodic, mixing Talking Heads and early The The, with Damon's vocals vacillating between David Bowie and mid-Atlantic Elton John. There were already indications of the later Blur sound with stabbing guitars, occasional brass riffs and complex structural forms. The highlights of the record were 'Elizabeth', 'Salvation', 'Happy House' and a track about the Queen called 'She Said'. Eddie was so convinced of Circus that he left his administrative job at Wembley Stadium to work on the band full time. "Graham really had done us a major favour. To this day it still amazes me how easily he took that situation on board."

With the recording complete, the band arranged a celebration party. Loads of friends were duly invited and the drinks flowed. Someone even brought a large bottle of Irish moonshine. Graham had invited some friends from Goldsmiths' College and one of them, Alex James, listened carefully to Circus' great masterpiece. "That's shit," he said. Far from being offended, Damon and Eddie were impressed by his nerve, and they spent the rest of the night getting blind drunk together on the 100% proof illicit Irish spirits.

Undeterred by Alex's comments, Circus continued rehearsing and producing demos, and were encouraged along the way by Steve Walters at EMI, who advised them to get out and gig. Circus played their first and only gig in Victoria Hall, Southborough in Kent, a show arranged by a friend of Eddie's wife. Supported by Whale Oil and Annie, it went very well. After this, and with spirits high, they went back to the studio to record yet more new material that Damon had written. But Eddie was in for a shock.

The new Circus material was light years away from anything they had done before, and there was even talk of changing the band's name to The Becketts. Eddie listened to it several times and came to a painful decision. At the next rehearsal he left. "One day we went from a melodic pop band to Dinosaur Jr with swathes of guitar over everything," he says. "It was a complete and very sudden change. It wasn't for me. That wasn't what I wanted from the band so I had to go." Despite the brave decision to leave his full time job, Eddie, along with bassist Dave Brolan, left Circus and formed The Shanakies, who went on to become The Apple, and whose paths would again cross with Damon, Graham and Dave in years to come.

The Shanakies / The Apple:

(Clockwise) Dave Brolan (with Guitar), Alain Maurel, Eddie Deedigan and Sam Bassu

Circus was down to a threesome of Damon, Graham and Dave Rowntree. Dave was nearly six years older than Graham, being born in Colchester Hospital on April 8,1963. His sister Sarah is five years older. His father worked for 40 years as a sound engineer at Broadcasting House, just up the road from the site of the Albarn's shop. Rowntree Senior even did some uncredited engineering work on The *Beatles At The BBC* album. With Dave's mother being in the London Orchestra, it was another very musical household. Dave's first instrument was a simple set of bagpipes given to him by his dad, who also introduced him to jazz, and enrolled him at Bob Coxon's weekend class. From there, Dave's musical interest blossomed, and by his teen years he was a very keen drummer.

Dave made his début at a street party during the 1977 Silver Jubilee celebrations, where along with a neighbour's son on piano, they performed an ear-splitting rendition of 'Yellow Submarine'. He also took drumming classes, where he was taught by a gargantuan Scotsman who taped a sixpence to the drum skin and hit Dave over the head every time he missed. Not overly academic, Dave attended a mixed grammar school where he adopted the unused school drum kit as his own, before heading for a HND in Computer Science at Woolwich Polytechnic.

By the time Damon and Graham were studying for their 'O' levels, Dave was 19, wearing a kaftan and long hair and answered to the nickname of Shady Dave. He bummed around Colchester bedsits for a while and finally formed Idle Vice, a three piece with his friend Robin on guitar and Jim on bass. The band moved to a Crouch End squat, and for six months entertained the London squat scene, playing hurried gigs at parties, mostly centred in and around King's Cross. Dave cropped his long hair into a thick black Mohican, and developed a worrying tolerance for huge quantities of cider. Then his wanderlust took over, so he upped and left for France, where he earned a meagre living

Opposite: Blur's penchant for stylish artwork was apparent even in their early days

for just over a year by busking and playing in small clubs.

Back in England and desperately short of money, he took a job as a computer programmer at the local council, complete with Mohican and shiny suit. He left Idle Vice and appeared to settle down until Damon asked him to join Circus. Dave liked the music and enjoyed the recording, but was disappointed to see Eddie and Dave Brolan leaving after their first gig. It was a major blow, especially as Damon and Eddie were such good friends, but they had to find replacements. Graham was more than capable of handling guitar duties alone. All that was missing was a bassist.

Alex James. Tall, dark, confident, and a lousy bass player. His first guitar, a Fender Precision copy was bought for £50 out of *Exchange & Mart* with money given to him on his 16th birthday, and was more of a fashion accessory than a musical instrument. He called his first band The Age Of Consent, and to impress his friends Alex spliced an introduction by him on to a few tracks by Fleetwood Mac, then told his mates it was his band. It worked until someone recognised the four Fleetwood Mac tracks. He never studied music, and was even kicked out of recorder class at primary school. Years later he offered an explanation: "My music teacher was eventually sent to prison for being a buttock fondler, which may explain why I never took the subject at school."

Alex was four months older than Graham, and spent much of his childhood in Bournemouth on Hampshire's south coast. He was born four years after his sister Deborah

in Boscombe Hospital on November 21. His father sold fork lift trucks and electronic rubbish compactors, and his mother did voluntary work. When his grandfather died, the James family moved into his guest house where they shared their life with a weird menagerie of pets. A £100 piano, bought for his eleventh birthday, inspired his desire for a keyboard, but since he couldn't afford one he opted instead for the bass.

The quiet retirement resort quickly frustrated the energetic Alex. Despite his boredom, he excelled at school with 13 'O' levels which were complemented by three top grade 'A' levels two years later. Before he headed off to college, he took a year out which included a job selling cheese at Safeway, where he developed his renowned taste for dairy products. He also worked as a labourer at Winfrith Nuclear Power Station, experimented with acid and was never short of female company. He also formed an ill-fated band called Mr Pangs Big Bangs (named after his landlord), but by the time he started at Goldsmiths' College he was relatively inexperienced in music.

Alex could have taken any subject at Goldsmiths' but he opted for French. On his very first day there, he saw Graham getting out of his parents' car with a guitar case under his arm, and went over and introduced himself. They became good friends, helped by the fact that their rooms were directly under one another in the Camberwell halls of residence.

For some reason known only to himself, Graham plastered his bedroom walls with Pixies lyrics on bright pink paper. Alex meanwhile initiated his own school of thought called 'Nichtkunst' into which he dragged Graham. It was an odd clique which largely involved staying up all night and drawing weird pictures, getting increasingly stroppy with each other as the sleepiness swept in and trying to convince themselves they were a movement to rival the Bauhaus. They weren't, but it was a laugh.

Damon first met Alex at the party when Alex told him Circus were shit. After this, the group of friends shared plenty of gigs, beers and acid. One show which stood out in all their minds was a legendary performance by The Happy Mondays at London's Astoria. Damon remembers this period well: "I used to go to loads of parties and when I got there Graham was always lying on the ground like a human doormat."

On one occasion after a night of especially copious drinking, following a show of Goldsmiths' students' work, Alex woke up the next day in the middle of a field in Kent, while Damon blacked out after two bottles of tequila and fell asleep in Euston station. The police rescued him and slung him in Holborn police cells, where he was brought round by a Nepalese soldier in full uniform. Tramps had stolen all his money so he had to walk home.

The Circus album had been recorded in January 1989 and by the spring term Eddie and Dave Brolan had left to form The Shanakies. Damon knew Alex played a little bass and so he asked if he fancied playing. "I thought Damon was a bit of a wanker but he had these keys to a studio so I joined," said Alex later. With the completed line up came a new name – Seymour.

VICTORIA HALL SOUTHBOROUGH

JAN
THURS
26th
8.00 P.M.

CIRCUS

What·Oi

£2.50

TICKETS: J.A.B's & THE PEACE SHOP

# 4

## Sing

Much confusion and uncertainty surrounds Seymour's first gig. Many believe it was at the Goldsmiths' show where their drunken debauchery put Damon in a cell for the night, but this was before Alex joined. There is also talk of a gig at a railway museum near a village outside Colchester. What is certain is that the actual line-up that eventually became Blur did not finally come together until the early summer of 1989, during Alex and Graham's second year at Goldsmiths'.

Uncertainty also reigns about the infamously bad name – perhaps it was taken from one of Damon's fictional characters, or indeed from a Salinger story of the same name. The latter is more probable since many of Salinger's characters, including his most celebrated fictional creation, Holden Caulfield, are downtrodden, alienated teenagers, and likely role models for aspiring art students.

Seymour's life was short, sweaty, but successful – within a year they had signed a record deal. Damon was churning out songs all the time and with a few regional shows under their belts they booked their first gig in London. They were supporting the excellent New Fast Automatic Daffodils and the dire Too Much Texas, at Camden's Dingwalls, and in anticipation they plastered the Underground with Seymour stickers.

It was a fashionable bill which attracted many music press and record company types, but the show ended badly for Seymour. After finishing their shambolic set, their drunken high spirits and a friend's willy waving unnerved a bouncer sufficiently for him to panic and spray mace in the band's faces. They stumbled out into the street, smarting from the spray and ended the night in hospital having their eyes checked. To add insult to injury, *Music Week*'s positive review was incorrectly spelt: "This unsigned and unheard of Colchester band played a blinder which swiftly endeared them to the Dingwalls disaffected. There could well be a gap in the goofy market and Feymour have the charm to fill it."

After this ignominious start, they gigged sporadically around the capital, including a support slot to the Swiss techno-meisters The Young Gods and third on the bill at The Lady Owen Arms to a band with an even worse name – Dandelion. At first, the only feedback was from Graham's guitar. At a Brighton Zap Club gig, Seymour even dabbled in performance art with odd-shaped boxes on stage (the support band for the night was an infant jangly Suede, complete with Justine Frischmann on rhythm guitar).

At this point, there was nothing to suggest that Seymour would evolve into the musically complex Blur. Graham was firmly immersed in a My Bloody Valentine/Dinosaur Jr fixation and noisy walls of sound that smothered everything. Damon was hunched over a second-hand keyboard adding to the racket, occasionally getting up to spiral wildly around the stage. Alex and Dave chipped in with some odd funky dance rhythms, which made Seymour sound like a weird cross between The Wolfhounds and Sonic Youth. It was

shambolic, unfocused, but not without promise. Damon loved it, and later told *Sky* magazine: "We just worked and worked on making ourselves brilliant. It's great being in a band when you're that age, thinking about what you want to be, doing manifestos, thinking about your image."

One record company man had tried to catch Seymour at Dingwalls, but couldn't get in because of the fashionable nature of the bill. Andy Ross was Head of Food Records, a nascent off-shoot of EMI and home to dance groovers The Soup Dragons and American success story Jesus Jones. The word was out that Seymour were a good live band, and Ross had already received a demo which showed some promise. Amongst the demo tracks were 'Tell Me, Tell Me', 'Long Legged', 'Mixed Up', 'Dizzy', 'Fried' and 'Shimmer', but it was the stand out song 'She's So High' that grabbed Ross' attention.

Still doubling as a journalist at *Sounds* magazine, Ross finally got to hear Seymour at an Islington Powerhaus gig in November 1989, and he was suitably impressed, as he told *Record Collector*: "They were crap but entertaining. Two better tracks on the demo showed that they had a clear grasp of the facets of simple songwriting. Everything was in the right place and in the right proportion." Ross couldn't deny that Seymour were something else live – the music may have been ramshackle but by now the band were dynamic on stage, and Damon in particular behaved like a man possessed. Ross saw Seymour twice more and then decided there was enough substance to offer them a contract. When they finally signed to Food Records in March of 1990 Seymour had played just ten gigs.

The deal was simple – Food would release their records and offer a £3,000 advance; Seymour would sign away world-wide rights, change their name and burn the grubby pyjama bottoms which Dave wore at gigs. The band signed. Graham and Alex never completed their degree courses – their finals were only two months away but they never went to College again. A proposed list of names discussed in a West End pizzeria included The Shining Path, Whirlpool, Sensitise and Blur. One option was a group of Peruvian revolutionaries and another was a brand of dishwasher. Ironically, a few weeks after signing someone discovered that a band called Blurt already existed and their second album was comically called *Kenny Rogers' Greatest Hits: Take 2*, but inquiries failed to track them down, and a possible name clash was avoided. All that was left was for Dave to vow never to wear his beloved pyjama bottoms again on stage. Record companies expect so much from young bands nowadays.

●　●　●

The spring of 1989 saw the beginnings of 'Madchester'. Inspired by the tradition of Manchester bands, notably Joy Division, New Order and A Certain Ratio, the movement was led by The Stone Roses with The Happy Mondays and Inspiral Carpets following closely behind. 'Baggy' music swept across the nation in a tide of flares, long sleeved loose fitting shirts and Joe Bloggs clothing. A general air of apathy seemed to characterise the scene. The bands took

lethargy-inducing drugs, were apolitical and shared an abstract dismay towards life in Britain. Peculiar to Manchester, the sound wasn't transportable, at least not overseas, and its proponents seemed almost disdainful towards stardom and the trappings of success.

By the end of the next year 'baggy' was creatively dead with the foremost proponents, The Stone Roses, locked in bitter courtroom struggles, spending their time in the dock rather than the charts. But 1989 was theirs, and Madchester was a genuine and far-reaching phenomenon. It was impossible for contemporary bands to ignore these events. Even though the creative death knell of baggy had largely been sounded by the time Blur signed to Food, the repercussions continued for some time to come.

Initially, Blur had wanted to release a single immediately after signing, but Ross convinced them it would be more beneficial to hit the road first to develop a ground swell of support. In July 1990, they headed out on a month long tour, taking in medium sized venues such as Walsall's Junction 10 and London's Tufnell Park Dome. The recklessness that had made Seymour such an attractive band to watch became even more frenzied. Damon's stage antics were increasingly dangerous. Jumping off speakers had graduated to climbing up lighting rigs and flaky ceilings, and this care-free abandon often bordered on the suicidal. The word spread and several promoters refused to book them. Conversely, the ticket-buying public could not get enough of it. "During this tour I think a lot of people came to see us just in case I killed myself," said Damon later.

Musically, Blur were much more accessible than their previous incarnation, as Alex told the press at the time: "Seymour was the more radical, non-bite sized, unfriendly face of Blur." Damon admitted that this transition to a more user-friendly sound was quite deliberate: "Seymour was our obtuse side. I didn't think we'd do well with our obtuse side, so we made less of it. Half our personality is latent."

Damon's destructive abandon set them apart from the baggy crowd, but many of the songs had a similar feel, so Blur were invariably tagged as hanging on to baggy's coat-tails. The Stone Roses comparisons were clear, and the legacy of Graham's My Bloody Valentine fixation was also strongly apparent. Blur were unimpressed by these parallels and complemented their live shows that summer with an arrogant press campaign that certainly got them noticed.

Blur's first public announcement was that they would not release a single until they had secured the front page of a weekly music paper. Their second was that they had no intention of slogging around the toilet venues of Britain for five years, and that their time was now. Their third concerned their début album – asked if this would happen soon, a spokesman for Blur said "We're going to be huge anyway, so why hurry?"

Damon in particular was always ready to mouth off about just how unique it all was, as this extract from *NME* shows: "I've always known I'm incredibly special, and if I didn't think we were the best band in the universe, I wouldn't bother." He was particularly dismissive of the baggy scene. "The difference is that Blur are going to be hugely successful." With the benefit of hindsight that sounds prophetic, but it is worth bearing in mind that Blur had yet to release a single, and for many people this pretty face was just another self-important upstart shooting his mouth off in the music press for easy headlines.

Nevertheless it seemed to work. Their gigs during the summer were all well attended and reviews were frequent and glowing, albeit littered with musical comparisons. T-shirt sales were high, and enquiries to Food about the début single steadily increased. In the first week of July, less than four months after signing their record deal, Blur won their first weekly front cover, when *Sounds* heralded them as one of Britain's best new bands alongside Ned's Atomic Dustbin and Senseless Things. The combined effect of the press coverage and compelling live shows fuelled Blur's rapid progression from tiny venues like Sir George Robey to a headlining slot at ULU to 1,000 people. This big autumn gig made Blur the first band to top the bill there before they had a record out. It was a flying start.

During these dates, Blur had been visiting Battery Studios (where The Stone Roses recorded 'Fool's Gold') in Willesden to begin work on the début single. The sessions were lengthy, often taking up to 18 hours a day, and two tracks, 'She's So High' and 'I Know', stood out. In contrast to many fledgling bands, Blur were looking for something very different from their records, as Damon told one magazine. "We have no intention of duplicating our live sound, the record should be something great, while live is more of an exhilarating thing."

The choice was eventually made and 'She's So High' nominated as the début single. Six weeks before its October 15 release, some white label promos were given to select club DJ's to whip up underground interest in advance. Produced by Steve Power and Steve Lovell (the latter having worked with Julian Cope), there was some friction in the studio over the band's musical ability – it took over a week to record just this one track. Power had doubts about Alex's playing and on one track he insisted Graham play bass, the ultimate insult to any musician. Damon sympathised with his band-mate's predicament: "Us three were as good as classically trained, so that puts Alex at a bit of a disadvantage, as we have that experience of sitting in orchestras and being shouted at and Alex doesn't."

Once released, 'She's So High' was a worthy début. Very much a product of the time, its languid dance feel and mellow tempo was in stark contrast to Blur live. The punk edge of their shows was relegated behind treacle guitar effects and sugary sweet harmonies. Graham had written some of the lyrics while Damon was sunning himself on holiday in Spain, but the nucleus of the song was inspired by a jam led by Alex. As such this track remains the most democratically created Blur song of all. It hit No.48 in the charts, despite a relative lack of radio airplay and a critical drubbing by Jonathan Ross on *Juke Box Jury*. Word of mouth was on Blur's side.

The music papers were more impressed than the record buying public, giving the record several 'Single Of The Week' accolades, although *Sounds* critic Leo Finlay was a little over-zealous in saying that "regardless of production, 'She's So High' stands comparison with anything of the last five years, Blur are the first great band of the Nineties." The B-side, 'I Know', was more reminiscent of Seymour and lyrically both tracks were nonsensical, although there were some vague references to drug culture and clubs in the lead tune. The vacuous banality of Damon's early lyrics is curiously at odds with his latter day reputation as a serious lyricist.

Interestingly, much of the attention for the single centred around the sleeve artwork. It was designed by Food's regular collaborators, Stylorouge, a design studio well experienced in record sleeve work, and it was the start of a long and fruitful relationship. The central image of a naked blonde sitting astride a hippo was taken from a Sixties painting by American pop artist Mel Ramoff (who Blur eventually met)

but the idiosyncratic style was lost on many people, who took exception to the sexist overtones. During their 21-date tour of Universities and Polytechnics to promote the single, Blur were frequently bombarded with protests about the sleeve image. At Coventry Polytechnic, The Steve Biko bar banned anyone wearing the corresponding Blur T-shirts, Warwick University students attacked the band's merchandise stall, Hackney Council complained to Food and in Brixton feminists ripped down Blur fly-posters. Some observers saw this as an indication of a much wider scam. With the name change, the Stylorouge design and the fashionably lolloping rhythms, they claimed that Blur were just a pre-fabricated Jesus Jones, the product of a shoddy hype campaign.

This was understandable, but did not allow for the extensive touring which put Blur in that position in the first place, nor the continued gigging that followed the release of the single. The promotional tactics might have stifled a lesser act, but Blur's live show at this time was their saviour. Gig after gig was lauded by an enthusiastic press. Damon's frenzied performances belied an intrinsic discipline and musicality within the band – Blur appeared always to be on the verge of collapse but they never actually did.

The lengthy single tour was topped off at Christmas by a support slot to the fleetingly successful Soup Dragons at the cavernous Brixton Academy. Although Blur had only been together for less than a year, the band took this huge 3,000 capacity gig in their laid back stride. It was a highly fashionable bill, maybe dangerously so, but Blur's punkish performance was so strong that one music paper reviewed only them, choosing to ignore the headliners. The show was a fitting end to a strong opening year.

Such was Blur's self-belief that they waited a full six months before putting out their second single. In the meantime they spent Christmas and the New Year in London social hotspots and wrote material for their first album. When the second single finally arrived, any fears that they may have lost the momentum were immediately erased when 'There's No Other Way' hit No. 8 in the charts. Again, Food had pre-released some white labels to the club scene eight weeks in advance, and the band even started a 17-date tour three weeks before its April release date. The song was blatantly derivative but so ultra-modern that it was a massive hit in the pop world. The beat itself was bang up to date, and Graham's snarling riff ricocheted all over the song. An infectious melody, snappy dance groove and memorable chorus fitted seamlessly into the flow of post-baggy songs then riding high in the charts .

With this new single, Blur skirted dangerously close to the fringes of baggy parody. The track was produced at Maison Rouge in Fulham by Stephen Street (who had worked with The Smiths and went on to produce The Cranberries) after the band met him in The Crown public house in the West End. It was the beginning of one of the most celebrated band-producer relationships in recent years.

Lyrically, the single was dreadful. Damon preferred to see this weakness somewhat more philosophically. "I don't claim that we are stunningly original, I firmly believe in just writing brilliant songs that have an incisive message," he wrote in a letter to *NME*. "I don't like using more than ten words in a song if I can help it, and then I can create a little ball of emotion." Vocally he wasn't excelling either – for "plaintive vocal" read "weedy and piss-weak". Graham grew to hate the song, and some time later he told *NME*: "It is a monumentally bland record, it's so banal. Its banality led to its being scrutinised when in fact it is about absolutely nothing. Making that record was like deliberately handing in this strange crappy essay at school just to see what people would think."

The Top 10 success of 'There's No Other Way' took Blur on to *Top Of The Pops* for the first time. "I have been preparing for this moment for years," said Damon pompously. Graham clearly hadn't – he couldn't get into the BBC and had a toe-to-toe row with a doorman. It was a shambolic, chaotic but endearing performance that exposed Blur to a nationwide audience for the first time.

In the weeks that followed, with the single still doing well, Blur attracted the attention of the tabloid press, with hilarious speculation about their private lives. The *Daily Mirror* called them 'Britain's Brainiest Band' (obviously they hadn't seen Damon's A-level results) while *The Star* chose to pursue the sex, sex and er, sex angle. Blur, they reported, shagged, drank, drugged, shagged some more and all before breakfast. Even Dave, unassuming chap that he is, was transformed into 'The Dark Destroyer'. Slots on the demonic *Terry Wogan Show* and a feature in *Woman's Own* were turned down, but Blur did appear on the kids Saturday

TV show *8:15 From Manchester* and in *Mizz, Smash Hits*, and many more nationwide publications and shows.

The teen mags picked up on Blur's good looks and poppy single and hailed them as one of Britain's most shaggable bands. The glossy magazines were crammed with fictitious trivia such as Damon and Alex's penchant for starting each day with a bottle of champagne and a shiatsu massage. The band apparently demanded cheese and port on contract riders, and required new underwear from a top London department store for each gig.

Such presumptions were designed to titillate and, ludicrous though they were, they brought in the girls. Blur's smiling features were soon Sellotaped on to many a bedroom wall. This was an important commercial cross-over in the making, and further fuelled the rumours of a pop scam.

This young following mixed with the older audience of the music weeklies to give Blur an unusual demographic following. At their smaller provincial gigs, the venues were filled with unusually young fans, with much screaming and general knicker-wetting excitement. For these fans the repressed punk tendencies of Blur came as a shock to ears used to hearing their sugary sweet pop singles. At the city shows, such as London's Town & Country Club, the audiences were more sombre, and older. Blur seemed to be genuinely straddling many age and culture groups.

The tour had to be expanded with another four dates to cope with demand, and was a complete sell-out (as some would say Blur were at this point). They toured the UK twice in the next four months and in London tickets were changing hands outside the venue for £50. Inside, the band's famous Penguin Classics T-shirts were selling by the crate-load. There was only one hitch. At the Woughton Centre gig in Milton Keynes, the band were banned from performing there ever again after Alex jumped into the crowd with his bass and smacked a young fan across the head, sending him to hospital with slight injuries in an apologetic tour manager's car. Despite Damon being a professional madman live, he issued a sensible statement, designed perhaps to placate worried mothers across the country: "We're not a mad irresponsible band. Our gigs don't usually end up in a blood bath. This was an isolated one-off accident and we're sorry about it."

Damon was always the most talkative in interviews, and also seemed the most sceptical. Concerning the enormous teen success of 'There's No Other Way' he said to *NME*: "I think it's inevitable when you are in our position and you look like we do that you're going to get seen as teeny idols. It's not something that we're keen to cultivate, but what can we do?" Dave was a little more enthusiastic: "I find myself waking up in the morning and realising what's happening to me and just thinking 'This is fantastic!' I still haven't properly come to terms with it yet."

Dave needn't have got too excited – with the band's third single 'Bang', they seemed to be trying to burst their own bubble. Perhaps finishing the album with Stephen Street distracted them; perhaps the fact it was written in only 15 minutes showed; perhaps the lacklustre, strained melody and weak harmonies suggested Blur might be a flash in the

pan after all. 'Bang' certainly did little for their cause and barely added to the expectation for the forthcoming album. Its only real plus was a distinct improvement in Alex's bass work. 'Bang' stalled at No. 24 in early August 1991, but at least their second *Top Of The Pops* performance was more memorable, with Damon parading around the stage waving a plastic cockerel, comically mimicking the theme of the sleeve art work.

Damon in a rare
moment of shoe-gazing

• • •

In 1992, Ride released *Going Blank Again*, which critics saw as an unofficial epitaph for yet another dying music movement, the awkwardly named Scene That Celebrates Itself. This had centred around a hub of bands who could be found at various trendy London watering holes, including The Syndrome Club in Oxford Street on a Thursday night , The Powerhaus, The Underworld and The Borderline. They were often seen at each other's gigs – Blur's studio party in Fulham to celebrate completing their album was attended by most of the leading lights of the scene. The collection of bands included under this umbrella was wide and varied but was generally accepted to be listless, apolitical and monosyllabic groups who were fairly inactive live and had little to say in their music, which was often swathed in Dinosaur Jr/My Bloody Valentine walls of noise, in sharp contrast to decidedly bland lyrics. It was different to baggy that's for sure, but it was not exactly life-affirming and eclectic.

Bands known as "shoe-gazers" (apparently a term christened by Andy Ross of Food to describe all those groups that Blur were *not* like) included Moose, Ride, Telescopes, The Boo Radleys, Lush, Chapterhouse, Slowdive and Blur. This was not a new experience to Blur – at the very start of their career, one writer had laughably tried to christen them as the leaders of 'The New Essex Scene', while another tagged them as the 'New Glam Lad Renaissance'.

More often than not, a band's inclusion was more to do with their ability to share a pint with a music journalist than with their musical style, and in this category Blur excelled. Throughout the spring and summer of 1991, Blur were regulars in both the trendiest bars and the juiciest gossip columns. One week they were pissed and loud here, the next they were, er, pissed and loud over there. Having yet to shake off accusation of baggy bandwagon-jumping, Blur now found themselves accused of joining this dubious bunch as well, and their reputation as professional music biz liggers (and open drug users) undermined their musical credibility. For many Blur were the Rent-a-lush of the current crop. Damon often seemed more than happy at their inclusion, as he told *Melody Maker*: "We have that idea of deliberate vagueness, of saying nothing and having a point to say nothing, It's that 'Blank Again' generation thing that we started, and were talking about nine months ago. There's a whole generation of bands that understand that every musical movement has failed to change anything, so we're deliberately shallow in order to avoid the embarrassment of it all."

After a while, the acclaim afforded to many of these bands began to ebb away, and as it did their friendly associations turned into back-stabbing and mutual disregard. Not all of the 'shoe-gazers' followed Blur into the charts, with only The Boo Radleys, Lush and Ride enjoying any longevity. Blur managed to survive through a mixture of sheer persistence and their awareness that any scene is of transitory benefit. Once Damon realised this, he was keen to distance Blur from the dying movement, as he told *Melody Maker*: "Bands like Ride, Chapterhouse and Slowdive had a wonderful pubescent quality, but they were sort of 'the end of indie', it had nowhere else to go."

• • •

Blur did have somewhere to go, their début album *Leisure*. Interest in the album was fuelled just before the late August release by a superb Reading Festival performance (which was unfortunately over-shadowed by Nirvana's triumph). *Leisure* was reasonably well received and did handsome commercial business, but it was a rather shambolic, unfocused affair, with two great singles, one poor one, and few other indications that Blur would progress. They had shown themselves more than capable of storming the singles charts and holding their heads up live, but albums were a different sphere, and with *Leisure*, Blur fell short.

One suggested title was *Irony In The UK*, but Blur plumped for *Leisure*, summing up the barely visible theme that tenuously linked the tracks together. The celebration of hedonistic youth, the love of life and music, and the obsession with enjoyment were Blur's manifesto. Lyrically, however, there was little clear embellishment of this central tenet. Damon was still producing painfully vague lines such as "Well, you must be mad, And you know you are, You should have known I'd do anything for you, so why, why?". Some critics talked of lovelorn angst, poetry and lyrical dreams but perhaps they were listening to a different album. The I/me focus hinted at a self-centred theme, but there was no real shape, it was all too generalised. Damon himself later admitted that he had actually written most of the lyrics five minutes before recording them – and it showed. He told *Q* magazine: "After *Leisure,* I had a very hard time, and rightly so, it was a shit album. There were a few good songs but I was an appalling lyricist, lazy, conceited, woolly."

Musically the record hardly broke away from the noisy MBV/Dinosaur Jr fixations of earlier material, and songs were often crammed with sustain and feedback at the expense of a discernible melody. The first two singles were there in all their pop glory, but elsewhere killer melodies were in short supply. Clumsy tracks like 'Fool', 'High Cool' and 'Come Together' cluttered the record and the lazy beats suddenly seemed dated. Backing tracks were largely done live, but the essence and energy of Blur live was absent. On the plus side, Graham added some interesting touches – the backward guitars on 'Sing' were achieved by actually learning the song backwards, note for note. Spatters of psychedelia – backward guitars, phased keyboards and drum samples – were everywhere which added interesting detail, but you can't polish a turd.

Maybe the lack of shape was due to the mix'n'match approach to production. Conflicting schedules meant that four separate producers were involved, and there were rumours that Stephen Street was called in to kick the band up the arse and get the lethargic project back on track. Even then, it was still a mish-mash, with several ancient Seymour tracks, including 'Birthday' 'Fool' and 'Sing'. The latter – an excellent, even daring ballad – was one of the few more adventurous highlights, a million melancholic miles from what people expected of Blur . The only other strong tracks were 'Repetition' with its waspy guitar and distorted vocals, and the closing 'Wear Me Down' complete with sugary threats, heavyweight guitars and a strong melody. Much of the record was swathed in noisy guitars which often clashed with Damon's lethargic, high-in-the-mix vocals. These swerved from Pete Shelley to Mick Jagger to Syd Barrett – intriguing enough maybe, but not when delivered in his weak Home Counties drawl. *Leisure* was, to be polite, "one for the fans."

At least there were plenty of those. The album sold very strongly, reaching No. 7. The £250,000 spent on the record was quickly recouped, a rare feat for many bands. Critically it was warmly received, although those writers who disliked it did so with a passion – Blur were rapidly becoming a love/hate band. Despite the generally strong reviews, it wasn't about to win any writing awards, but Blur were always very aware of this. Shortly after *Leisure,* Damon told *Select:* "*We* shouldn't be judged on those songs and those performances. We were a fledgling group having a laugh, but we didn't have a particular agenda." He also called himself "a dyslexic illiterate." Graham's infamous comment that it was their "indie de-tox album" perhaps sums it up better than any. This was Blur enjoying their initial success, not worrying too much about focus, just finding their feet in the band, and in that respect it was engaging enough.

Blur were giving early hints that their next album might not be so linear, that they were already plundering their environment for inspiration: "We're all products of our backgrounds and environment, so what we produce is a product of that," said Damon. "We're influenced by adverts and Sunday magazines and slogans around us, things people say in films and certain moments , strange stances and gestures – the madness of human behaviour."

Part of the band's anxiety to suggest they were already moving on was to avoid being dragged down with the carcass of Madchester. With The Stone Roses grounded by legal problems and The Happy Mondays about to split, the movement had lost its two leading lights. Baggy ultimately became a term of abuse reserved for the likes of The Bridewell Taxis, which actually made a mockery of the movement's original ideas. Damon was obviously acutely aware of these developments and managed to distance Blur from the fall-out, He told *Select*: "The next album will be the start of an era. This one is the 'kill baggy' album."

To increase the suspense, Damon also offered a long term outlook that did not need to concern itself with the short-term benefits of a smash début album. "Blur isn't just a one-album phenomenon; it's something that has to develop over five or six years before we can get any sort of perspective." So, despite all the reservations about *Leisure,* they could have done a lot worse. Look at The Farm.

# 5

## Wear Me Down

With a commercially successful, recouping début album under their belts and a sell-out tour ahead of them, Blur might have reasonably expected a clear road ahead. Unfortunately, by the summer of 1992 the band were a shell of their former self, with in-fighting, drunkenness and indiscipline rife. Between now and then it was all downhill.

The 13-date album tour was critically well-received and tickets flew out, even for the bigger shows like Kilburn National. The gigs were now much more punk than sugary pop, as Damon told *Puncture*: "We're more aggressive and much more sensual than we are on record. We play the songs about four times as fast. It's like we have a mixture of tantrums and ecstasies on stage. It's very violent at certain points, and quite sexy at others."

Blur live and Blur on record were virtually two unrelated bands at this stage. Some critics hated them, such as *Melody Maker* writer Andrew Mueller who wrote: "In a year they will be seen as a Vapour for the Nineties, they really do mark the point at which this year's collective enthusiasm for the new has gone beyond a joke." Others loved them, and most agreed that the gigs, if musically erratic, were still strangely watchable.

In addition to their own album tour they performed on the Radio 1 *Roadshow* in Skegness in front of 20,000 kids and nine million listeners, they did PAs on more kids TV shows and then rounded off the year with their slot on the Food Records Christmas Party at Brixton Academy, alongside Diesel Park West, the label-named Sensitise and Whirlpool, and headliners Jesus Jones. The first 2,000 punters were given a free tape with two tracks by each band, including Blur's demo version of 'Resigned' and a re-mixed 'High Cool'. Special guest on stage for keyboard duties was Natasha of The Bikinis, and Damon managed to badly bruise his shoulder with his customary hands-behind-his-back human pinball routine.

Backstage at Rollercoaster, 1992

There were also a handful of dates in America, where the USA were briefly flirting with 'Madchester', and some French and Japanese gigs as well. Damon was not about to get carried away, however, as he told *Sky* magazine: "All you need to be mobbed in Japan is to have blonde hair and be more than five feet tall. Being mobbed is so... unrefined."

Blur's live reputation was acknowledged in the New Year of 1992 when they were offered a slot on the so-called 'Rollercoaster' tour. This was the brainchild of The Jesus & Mary Chain, based on Perry Farrell's hugely successful Lollapolooza tour in the USA. The American precedent had seen a rich diversity of bands including Jane's Addiction, Nine Inch Nails, Ice T, Living Colour and The Butthole Surfers on the same bill, along with performance artists and campaign stalls. The 'Rollercoaster' idea was somewhat more limited, with just four bands and no peripheral activities, but the motive was the same – put on an attractive bill of several bands for the price of most normal shows.

The Jesus & Mary Chain's first choices were Blur, Dinosaur Jr and My Bloody Valentine, which in retrospect limited the musical variety immediately, but there was still no denying it was probably the most attractive touring line-up for years. Blur were delighted and accepted straight away. Damon told *Melody Maker*: "Without wishing to sound really crap, I think 'Rollercoaster' is the most exciting thing we've done. We usually look to the next two weeks on the road with a sense of dread and loathing, but none of us can wait to get on this tour. To be honest, I'm a bit star-struck by it all. I'm delighted that we are gonna be playing with them, even though we're very different to all of them in our outlook and the way we try to present ourselves."

Blur were a relatively lightweight pop band on a rock bill, and several eyebrows were raised at their selection, even those of MBV's Kevin Shields. Nevertheless, Blur's slot also conferred on them a degree of levity and respectability that forced people to listen to them again. The gigs were massive – Birmingham's NEC, Manchester's Apollo and London's Brixton Academy were all sold out. This was the Mary Chain's first UK dates for two years and all four acts were capable of pulling a sizeable crowd.

Unfortunately 'Rollercoaster' quickly became something of a doom-fest. The Mary Chain headlined each night, with the other three bands rotating. This meant that if Blur came on first, the punter was then subjected to a prolonged blast of Dinosaur Jr/MBV/J&MC, enough gloom to out-gloom even the most morbid of music fans. Some dates were all seated and this stifled the atmosphere. Also, Blur were the only band seemingly willing to party backstage, and there was always a polite awkwardness between the four groups. Added to that the lack of an agenda, with none of the bands proselytising like Ice T might have, and the dates assumed an air of lethargy, of little historical significance other than value for money. This was no new rock dawn. Damon had told *Melody Maker*: "I think Rollercoaster is really important, the best thing that's happened to British music in a long time." Admirable enthusiasm, but it just wasn't to be.

Most reviewers saw Blur as superficial pop that was grossly out of place on this bill, and Damon's arrogance

continued to rub writers up the wrong way. He had only recently said: "We're a band who could completely and utterly change everything. The scale that we are working on is so enormous, we're trying to reach absolutely everybody." At this point in time, this sounded ludicrous. During the tour Blur also started to plan their first long form video, a documentary about provincial England to be directed by Storm Thorgeson (who had provided footage as a stage backdrop for each Blur song during the tour). A partner in the groundbreaking Hypgnosis design team, Thorgeson had conceived much of Pink Floyd's album art and many of their stage effects. A product of the Cambridge scene that spawned the Floyd, he was an old ally of the doomed Syd Barrett, and Blur were delighted to be involved with him. They planned to show the piece on Channel 4 but the actual video never materialised. Within weeks of finishing the 'Rollercoaster' tour, Blur realised it had probably done them more harm than good.

● ● ●

When a band are playing well and the crowd is loving it, constant drinking and debauchery is romanticised into 'partying'. When they are playing dreadful gigs night after night and arguing all day, it is called self-destructive abuse. When Blur hit the United States in May 1992 for a colossal 44-date, state by state tour, their drinking was already dangerously way out of control, and things just got worse.

In America Blur were simply a British oddity, and a drunken one at that. Since their last visit, the infant grunge had taken hold and Nirvana's *Nevermind* had sold nine million copies, so slacker culture was everywhere. Seattle, grunge, Eddie, Kurt, Hole and Sub Pop were the words on everybody's lips. To millions of disenchanted American kids

enlivened with the new teen spirit, Damon's cockney charm and Blur's English sound were utterly pointless. Blur were about as akin to grunge as Brett Andersen is to weight lifting.

This universal indifference exacerbated Blur's drunken indiscipline so much that they became a band just waiting to implode. Three gigs in and Damon's water-throwing antics caused the owners at The Venus De Milo theatre to pull the plugs after the just three songs. A small scale riot ensued with the band escaping out of a back door, followed by angry fans and even angrier security men chasing them down the street. A sense of impending doom dominated the tour bus, and in-fighting erupted daily. Within one three-day spell, each member of the band had thumped another, even Damon and Graham. Damon said to one journalist: "We don't really go into big violent moods with each other, but we're incredibly cruel to each other all the time, non-stop. We are cruel to the point where most people can't believe how awful we are to each other, just vicious, spiteful, it's mental torture, psychological warfare." This was rapidly becoming an American nightmare. Graham was unwell, with recurrences of ulcers and bleeding he had suffered on tour before, and Damon was constantly dragging on his high tar banana skin and clove Caravan cigarettes. On their way to the now hallowed grunge capital of Seattle, Blur's tour van broke down and they ended up spending hours in a run-down greasy spoon called The Potato Shop.

Their paranoid state was worsened by their American record company's attitude. SBK were determined to break the band state by state, and only gave them a meagre two days off in 44. Even when Blur played well, the American

press ridiculed them as yet another post-baggy Manchester band well past their sell-by date. The cumulative effect of the drinking, the American public's indifference, the media's ridicule and the record company's reckless work ethic was disastrous. By the end of the dates, tension in the band was high. Graham was told to lay off alcohol for six months and was rumoured to have been committed to a rest home to recuperate. Throughout the tour, all of the band came close to being, or actually were, hospitalised. On their return, Blur were a pathetic, drunken shambles. Damon told *NME* he was bitter about the way some tried to trivialise their terrible experience: "It makes me laugh when people describe that as rock'n'roll behaviour. It wasn't an affectation with us. When things are going well, I don't behave like that."

The saving grace in this mess should have been Blur's fourth single 'Popscene' released in March 1992, a song which had been débuted back at the Manchester Apollo the previous year. It was the first fruit of their post-*Leisure* sessions and was produced by Steve Lovell again, as Stephen Street was out of favour with Food's Dave Balfe. It is rather easy to see the brassy horn-driven chorus, the blazing fast melody and decidedly English feel of 'Popscene' as a long lost sign of great things to come. It was certainly a change in direction. The twitching riffs, choppy dynamics and energy were charming, and Blur's first use of a brass section was a sign of things to come. In certain reference points there were hints of Blur's imminent anglophile preoccupations, with clear similarities to The Teardrop Explodes and The Sex Pistols among others. The dog on the cover, taken from *Horse & Hounds* magazine, the lyrical slight on the British music business and the sense of nostalgic Englishness were all there. 'Popscene' was miles away from the ambient abstractions of shoe-gazing or the dated rhythms of baggy. It was a very Nineties song, a big departure, and possibly one of the first Britpop songs.

However, the single is now remembered because back then it was largely forgotten. Much has been made of 'Popscene' since Blur's massive success, but it is important to remember that at the time of its release it was absolutely and almost universally reviled. To a press and public similarly fixated with grunge, a 'kill baggy' combo's new single was completely uninteresting and the record was given short shrift in the papers. *Melody Maker* said it was… "a directionless organ-fest in search of a decent chorus". 'Popscene' was lost in the fashionable sea of lacerated vocals and serrated guitars.

At the time, the general critical indifference that met 'Popscene' could probably have been tolerated, but the commercial failure of the single was a devastating blow. It was Blur's first single for nearly a year, coming off the back of a Top 10 album, yet it stalled badly at only No. 32 and crashed out of the charts after only two weeks. The band and Food Records were stunned. Well-laid plans for the poppier 'Never Clever' to follow up 'Popscene' were abandoned. Worse still, the band had an album almost ready for release on their return from their US dates, but in the face of such indifference, Food said it would now have to wait.

Had this album been released, it would have contained many of the songs that subsequently appeared on *Modern Life*, with some B-sides that finally surfaced on future Blur singles such as 'For Tomorrow'. Damon said to *NME*: "We knew it was good, we knew it was better than what we had done before. We put ourselves out on a limb to pursue this English ideal and no-one was interested."

Dave was convinced it was a crucial track: "It was completely ignored by the press, but I think it was the point we realised we weren't going to listen to anything anyone else was saying. We knew then we were capable of making great records."

Coinciding with the dreadful American tour, the single's failure sent Blur spiralling into more depression, but despite their disappointment at the time, the refusal of Food to put the album out in 1992 and the failure of 'Popscene' were very possibly blessings in disguise. Had the second album come out during the grunge domination, it may well have lost all its impact and Blur would not have been able to establish the ground swell of support that provided the vital foundation for *Parklife*. Nevertheless, at the time the band was devastated.

Their misery was compounded by the discovery that their manager had pilfered most of the funds from *Leisure*. Blur hardly had enough money to pay the rent. Bankruptcy was only narrowly avoided. The Jesus and Mary Chain/Midge Ure manager Chris Morrison was brought in at the last minute, and he secured a Stateside merchandise deal that just about kept the band's heads above water.

There was worse to come. While Blur had been boozing their way around the States, back in Britain Suede had arrived. Heralded by an infamous *Melody Maker* cover announcing 'The Best New Band In Britain', Suede were critically lauded and plastered over every music magazine and paper. While Blur were disastrously flying the flag abroad, Suede had sneaked in and usurped them as the next big thing. It was the start of a long rivalry between the two

Suede

bands. Blur felt Suede's cockney slant and camp charm were plagiarised from themselves.

There were personal frictions as well, with Damon's girlfriend Justine Frischmann having been both a former rhythm guitarist in Suede (some say she invented the name) and an ex-girlfriend of Brett Andersen, the "bisexual who hasn't had a homosexual experience". Slanging-matches disgraced the music press, with Bernard Butler quoting lyrics from 'Bang' as his worst ever, and Damon constantly ridiculing Brett. Graham said Bernard Butler stole his style of guitar playing and that "he spent hours crying on my doorstep for us to take him on tour as a roadie." Alex said: "Brett got his impetus from Damon coming along and nicking his bird, now he had an axe to grind."

A source who worked closely with Suede at the time confirms this: "Many of the songs on Suede's début album were about Justine and Brett's relationship, that split-up was a big spur to him. 'Metal Mickey', 'Animal Lover' 'Moving' and 'To The Birds' were all highly focused on that situation. 'Pantomime Horse' was as well, but that has been dramatically misunderstood and misread. Most people see the lyric "Have you ever tried it that way?" as some kind of homosexual reference. It wasn't, not at all. It was about losing his girlfriend to Damon and looking at it from the other side of the fence. Suede's material improved considerably once Justine had left, no comparison."

Brett Andersen came to personify Blur's difficulties, but that did not excuse Damon's subsequent allegations that Brett was a heroin user (whether true or not), which took this rivalry to a new low. Damon later regretted this statement, telling *NME:* "Every time I got drunk I got very nasty about Suede, I just couldn't see the woods for the trees because of Justine." For now, however, he hated them and his frustration continued to grow and soon encompassed any band who were selling more records than Blur, which at this point was just about any band in the Top 30.

To make matters worse, it was a no-contest. Suede were winning all the honours and Blur were just a band in dire trouble. Suede were soon to be Brat award winners, Brit award nominees, Mercury Music Prize winners and Glastonbury highlights. Blur were nominated for nothing and were often so pissed they did well to turn up at some gigs. When they did show, as Damon recalls… "it had got to the stage where we were drinking so much we could hardly play our instruments."

The downward spiral could not continue much longer. Things had to come to a head, and they did at a July Gimme Shelter charity gig at London's Town & Country Club. In one night, the tour problems, the drinking, the arguing, the S**de word and the failure of 'Popscene' exploded in one huge mess. Blur shared the bill with guitar noise-mongers 31/2 Minutes, pop tune-smiths Mega City Four and the dreaded Suede. The socially motivated gig should have been Blur's comeback, snatching their crown back from the rival upstarts but things did not start well when Suede played a blinder. Backstage, Mega City Four were waiting to go on after Brett's band when Damon walked into their dressing room uninvited, swigging drunkenly from a bottle and mouthing off about America.

Singer Wiz recalls: "He was really pissed and going on and on about what it's like to be in a band, but especially about how shit America was and how it was great to play the bigger venues there 'cos you are miles away from the punters. He just kept saying he hated the place, he thought all Americans were wankers, and he fucking hated gigs, and he was trying to get us to agree. We just sat there listening, and I remember thinking 'we are not from the same planet as you' and then one of our band just opened the door, pointed him towards his own pissed-up dressing room and shoved him out."

**Backstage with Justine**

The band had been drinking all day and matters deteriorated when Damon walked on and said: "We're so fucking shit you may as well go home now." A few songs into Blur's piss-poor set and some people did. They made matters worse for casual observers by playing B-sides and demo tracks. Those that stayed were treated to the morose spectacle of a band committing public suicide. While Brett's hammed-up gender-bending Bowie-isms had been rapturously received, all Damon could manage was to pretend the mike was his dick and to bang his head on the speaker. He even got into a scuffle with a security guard – he looked like a prat, and the band played like novices. Blur's arrogant statements of the last two years now caught up with them with embarrassing effect. Keith Cameron in *NME* summed it up perfectly, as "Carry On Punk rock". The only difference is that Carry On films were funny.

The next morning Damon was awoken from his drunken slumber by an angry Dave Balfe of Food Records, who demanded a meeting that day. Balfe told him he had seen it all before with his band The Teardrop Explodes, the in-fighting, the excess, the over-indulgence, the bitterness. In short, he thought Blur were over. He gave them a month to sort themselves out or they would be dropped.

# 6

## Getting Snarled Up In The Suburbs

From this all time low, things could only get better. During the summer and early autumn of 1992, Blur tried to repair the physical, mental and financial damage they had suffered over the last eighteen months. Gradually, thoughts began to turn to new material and the band holed up in Maison Rouge to try to regain some focus and composure. The resulting second album, *Modern Life Is Rubbish*, actually fared worse than their début commercially, and enjoyed far less media coverage, but it was a watershed release. Even though many of the ideas were not complete, *Modern Life Is Rubbish* was a crucial sign of intent.

At first things had to get worse before they could get better. With Blur talking up an English theme for the new record, the quintessential post-punk Englishman Andy Partridge of XTC was chosen to produce the sessions (Stephen Street was still out of favour with Balfe). Ex-Eurythmic Dave Stewart's Church Studios in Crouch End were used for the sessions, but they were disastrous. Things began badly when Damon introduced himself by telling the producer how brilliant 'Making Plans For Nigel' was – a track actually written by Partridge's ex-XTC cohort and now-rival Colin Moulding. The band were still drinking profusely and they disliked his studio approach. Asked by XTC biographer Chris Twomey when it all started to go wrong Partridge said: "When they picked up their instruments and started playing! It wasn't totally successful. We didn't seem to hit it off, I think I am a bit dictatorial, I know what I like and I don't think they were delivering what I thought they were capable of. Maybe they thought I was pushing them a bit too hard. Maybe it was the 'difficult second album syndrome' for them."

Only three Blur tracks were recorded at these ill-fated sessions, 'Sunday Sunday', 'Seven Days', and 'Coping' as well as an ill-advised cover of Buggles' 'Video Killed The Radio Star' but none ever surfaced. Blur felt Partridge was trying to mould them into another Jesus Jones, and they were suspicious of Balfe's commercial motives (they later wrote 'When The Cows Come Home' specifically about Balfe's approach). They refused to use the sessions and Balfe was furious. Meanwhile, Graham had bumped into Stephen Street at The Marquee during a Cranberries gig and Blur began to push for his reinstatement as producer. At least with *Leisure* having recouped, Blur enjoyed a degree of independence many of their peers sorely missed.

Balfe eventually acquiesced and so their fruitful relationship was renewed. It was late autumn 1992 by now and recording went so well that the album was complete by just after Christmas. However, they still weren't in the clear yet – when Blur took the tracks to Balfe in the New Year, he rejected them, requesting at least another two singles. Damon was stung by the criticism, but went away and wrote the tracks the next day, calling them 'For Tomorrow' and 'Chemical World'.

Before the public got a taster of the new material, Blur played a low key one-off gig at the Fulham Hibernian, supported by the most unlikely of musical opposites – the fashionably PC but soon to be redundant Huggy Bear and The Salvation Army Band. At the show, a select number of free one-sided copies of a track called 'The Wassailing Song' were given away to 400 lucky punters. The rest of the nation had to wait until the new single in April.

The importance of 'Popscene' in Blur's rebirth has been overemphasised. Their next single, 'For Tomorrow', is actually of greater significance, despite also being a commercially muted affair. Without 'For Tomorrow', Balfe refused to accept the album and Blur's difficulties could have continued indefinitely. It was a considerable progression from Blur's previous work, even 'Popscene'. Coming after nearly a year's absence, there was considerable pressure, particularly since their last effort had failed so spectacularly. Damon himself raised the stakes by calling the new single "a 'Waterloo Sunset' for the Nineties", but this time his confidence seemed justified (albeit a little exaggerated). It was a melancholic tale of London life, complete with killer 'la la la' chorus, and it is ironic that Damon's biggest lyrical breakthrough should come with such a line.

Suddenly, Damon was a worthy lyricist – his vision of the contrast between romanticised London and the grim Westway of reality conjured up visions of grey tower blocks and modern day grimness. Damon reinforced his new vision with a spoken piece laid over the closing choruses which spoke of Primrose Hill, London ice, and Emperor's Gate. Vocally he rose from the plaintive dregs of shoe-gazing and baggy to assume a controlled arrogance that was surprising and highly appropriate. Against this, the music sound-tracked his new theme ideally, with weird twists on music hall melodies, finely detailed guitars and adept bass lines. The simple drum structure and string arrangements added a lush depth to its bare simplicity. Hooked together by a classic pop chorus, it was a blinding comeback, Blur's first

epic record in four years of trying. It was to be a single of pivotal importance.

Oddly enough, on its release in April 1993 'For Tomorrow' reached only No. 28, so in many senses it was as much a commercial flop as 'Popscene'. The video promo was directed by *Absolute Beginners* director Julien Temple but this failed to incite extra sales. Crucially however, Blur were not plunged into a spiral of destruction as they had been after the commercial death of 'Popscene'. They were convinced their new focus was valid and that the already-completed album would open up a future for them only hinted at by 'For Tomorrow'.

The core of this fresh angle was immediately apparent with the photo sessions for the new project, entitled 'British Image No. 1'. Blur were no longer pretty faced, bowl-haired teen idols – instead they wore turned up jeans, Fred Perry shirts and red Dr. Martens, with sharp suits and trimmed hair, and they shared the photograph with a huge Great Dane. When Blur went on a photo shoot for a weekly paper in an old Jag as well, it brought back memories of The Dave Clark Five, but they were casting their net much further than that. There had been hints of the new Blur at both the Reading and Glastonbury festivals of 1992, where the sharp suits and some new songs were previewed. However, the real extent of their new focus only became fully apparent on the release of their second album, *Modern Life Is Rubbish*. They'd had the germ of the idea for some time, and many of the tracks for months – it was worth the wait.

The band set their stall out on the inner sleeve with an oil painting of them on the Underground in full 'British Image No. 1' regalia. Through a mixture of infectious pop tunes, dark melancholic ballads, and a lyrical progression equivalent to Roger Hargreaves winning the Booker prize, Blur produced an album that made *Leisure* seem like someone else's record. Thematically, lyrically, musically and visually, *Modern Life Is Rubbish* was nothing short of a rebirth.

The British focus was the crux of the whole transformation. The album was originally going to be called *England vs. America*, and then *British Life 1*, but both were disposed of in favour of *Modern Life Is Rubbish* which the band felt was more universal and reflected the themes in the album more accurately (the actual phrase was taken from a piece of graffiti on a wall near to Marble Arch). Yes, there had been elements of that on *Leisure* and more hints with the brassy Englishness of 'Popscene', but it had never been articulated to this degree before. This was a very English record, peculiarly London-centric, and unashamedly so.

Lyrically Damon was unrecognisable. Some credit for that must go to girlfriend Justine (whose own band Elastica would soon start to take off) who frequently scolded Damon for his lyrical laziness and pointed him towards her enormous record collection. The spoken paragraph that closed 'For Tomorrow' was just the start – the whole record was a London montage full of the Underground, the Portobello Road, traffic jams, peeping Toms, adverts, commuters, check-out girls and the rush hour. Damon sang about Sunday colour supplements, Sunday roasts,

McDonald's and sugary tea, *Songs Of Praise* and Mother's Pride. While grunge ranted on about self-loathing and anti-consumerism (even though it was utterly consumerist itself), Damon was singing about catching a bus into the country, Essex man and the joys of Saturday markets. The English suburban malaise was viewed with a mixture of fascination and regret, as he introduced us to a range of characters, relationships and rituals through a predominantly narrative style. From being a lazy, reticent bystander, he was now a biting social commentator.

Vocally Damon dipped into several record collections for inspiration. Julian Cope, Bowie, and every band who had ever sung with a London accent were cited by the media and those influences are clear to see. At least he had dropped the awful reedy whine of the début album, and the deeper maturity gave his voice a serenade-like quality.

Musically, *Modern Life* was a complex yet direct album, and a veritable pop encyclopaedia. The array of instruments at last drew on the band's technically trained past, with amongst others a Solina organ, timpani, sleigh bells, Casio keyboards, drum box, Moog and melodica somewhere in the mix. To enrich the scenario still more, Blur also used other unusual sonic tricks, including a shopping PA system, a Butlin's tannoy, a typewriter bell, a triangle and even a Black & Decker drill. Graham's guitar work was now free of his MBV fixation, while Alex had also developed enormously. Dave was improving too, his precise drumming nailing Blur down to an infallible beat. Pop took second place to punk, with songs like the storming 'Advert' taking centre stage. There were pub knees-ups with 'Intermission', acoustic moods with 'Blue Jeans' and soft smooches with 'Miss America'. The instrumental variety maintained the level of interest throughout, and was cheekily rounded off by the two daft instrumental tracks that ended each side, 'Intermission' and 'Commercial Break'. Both were strong hints of future work and older influences. There were, of course, dull moments such as 'Resigned' and the lyrically questionable 'Villa Rosie' but these were in the minority.

Tambourine man

This musical mélange created a very parochial sound and Blur would henceforth be plagued by constant and largely justifiable press references to those British groups who expressed their nationality in song. Blur fit neatly into a lineage of clipped British pop. In *Modern Life* you can hear traces of Madness on 'Sunday Sunday', The Kinks on 'For Tomorrow', Buzzcocks on 'Colin Zeal' and The Smiths on 'Blue Jeans'. To claims that Blur were just recycling the past, Damon had a perfect answer. As the Nineties were built on mountains of precedent, no band could possibly be completely original, he claimed. He was cleverly excusing Blur from claims of retrogression, telling *NME*: "*Modern Life* is the rubbish of the past. We all live on the rubbish, and because it's built up over such a time there's no need for originality any more. There are so many old things to splice together in infinite permutations that there is absolutely no need to create anything new."

While their first album had followed prevailing trends, complete with incumbent baggy beats and phased guitars, *Modern Life* established new ideas from old. Blur were now scouring the musical past, taking pieces from here and there as required, covering almost everything from music hall to electro pop, as long as it was English. It was a record inspired and heavily immersed in another time and yet paradoxically was a very modern album.

In May 1993 the most unfashionable thing to release was an intensely Anglophile concept record, full of English suburban detail, based around a third person narrative of everyday life, and mixed with a distaste for all things American. That is exactly what *Modern Life* was. It should be acknowledged not because it pays homage to the likes of The Small Faces, The Kinks, and Madness, but because it did *not* draw from Led Zeppelin, Neil Young and all of the godfathers of grunge. Maybe the album will not be remembered as Blur's finest, but it is certainly their bravest.

● ● ●

Unfortunately, not everyone was convinced. The album was released to a mixed critical response, although most reviewers did at least acknowledge the progress made since their last long player. As with their previous two singles, the album did not fare that brilliantly in the charts, reaching No. 15 then dropping out of the listings three weeks later. By now Blur were too involved in their own world to notice. Sure, they were disappointed, but they couldn't help but feel positive. The corresponding press campaign was low key, with only one cover feature, but the articles that were published dramatically underlined Blur's new stance. In fact, Damon's increasingly accomplished interview technique meant that he quite often articulated the germ of an idea more proficiently in the media than on the actual record.

He explained that their dreadful American experience had been the creative catalyst for this album, and that the endless shopping malls and bubble culture appalled him almost as much as the Americanisation of England he saw back at home. Damon told *Puncture*: "America wasn't an option, so we concentrated on our own identity. We had started on the long road of odd pop." Through the drunken haze of that terrible US tour, the country had seemed all the more bloated and superficial, and by the time they arrived back in Blighty they loathed America, as he told *NME*: "We have stretched our sound considerably. When we were in America, England became this wonderful, fantasy place. The album is a soundtrack for a fantasy London, covering the last 30 years." He also told *Melody Maker*: "It really fascinates me now. I've really got into the idea of narrowing everything down to the Englishness of everything we do, so everything has much more force because it holds more relevance. You're deliberately focusing on what you know and what you are as a result of your conditioning. It's just an idea of paring yourself down to what you really are. This is a fascinating time to be English and it's great to have things around that focus."

Other articles saw Blur spray-painting the album title all over London and over a Clacton band stand, and Damon announcing "Modern life is rubbish is the most significant comment on popular culture since 'Anarchy in the UK'". Damon was clearly proud of being English, and disliked what he called the "coca-colonisation" of his home country.

Perhaps most controversially of all, in a *Melody Maker* piece by The Stud Brothers entitled "The Empire Strikes Back" Damon said: "I'm not saying that everyone should put on a fake Cockney accent and sing about the Old Bull & Bush, but I do feel that our culture is under siege and we are losing it." This article coincided with the election of BNP candidate Derek Beakon to an east London council and a growing fear of resurgent fascism. Damon carried on undeterred: "We should be proud of being British and not simply follow what comes from America." As examples he cited Olde Worlde pubs saying: "It's just like Britain has become a holiday camp full of cutesy British people. The pubs have become a real plastic replica of what they once actually were." He also slated American music by saying "Don't tell me Nirvana have changed the face of American rock. No-one should kid themselves that anything happens in America unless the establishment thinks there is a buck in it for them. I'm fed up with people taking over the world on the back of that crass nonsense. And what have they got to say for themselves? 'I'm fucked up'. Fantastic." Just in case some people hadn't got the point, Damon also said: "We killed baggy with our first album, this one will kill grunge."

Like it or not, it was gripping stuff. This was all a very long way from the early days of Blur celebrating superficiality as an art form. The thematic change and contentious statements whipped up yet another controversy around Blur – some sensed the image change was just another thinly veiled attempt to manipulate the media just like the promotional scams at the time of 'She's So High'. Others were unconvinced that such a stylistic change could be genuine, although Paul Weller publicly backed the band.

Elsewhere, the "Empire Strikes Back" article in particular incited a barrage of readers' letters for and against Blur's

stance. Many knee-jerk observers myopically talked about Blur flirting with fascism, just as Morrissey had done with disastrous results when he supported Madness at Finsbury Park. Others saw it as intended, a genuine attempt to seize back the initiative from the all-conquering Americans. At the same time, there was no denying the slightly thuggish look to the new image. Damon himself recognised the dangers , but felt their sincere intentions would show through. Still, the band turned down a front cover of *Scooter* magazine and refused offers to play at scooter rallies for fear of inciting the wrong kind of following, a problem that had plagued Madness for years. Besides, the album was not unreservedly pro-Britain anyway, as he told *NME*: "It doesn't hail England as some Utopian place. It doesn't say England is a place of growth and happiness, there is an underlying decay." In many senses *Modern Life Is Rubbish* was as much about a dying country as a vibrant one.

Regardless of commercial success or failure, the underlying premise of the new album was central to Blur's very survival: "We had to make *Modern Life* and we were disappointed when no-one got it. It was certainly the moment when things turned and we pulled ourselves together. We literally had very little to lose." He also revealed to *Select* that "*Modern Life* was the beginning of us having an idea of what we wanted to do. If we hadn't lost all our money we wouldn't have made the album so quickly but it worked." Damon seems to have an unerring ability to stand outside and observe the current musical climate, and this is possibly one of Blur's greatest strengths. With alarming accuracy, and at a time when Kurt Cobain could do no wrong, Damon recalls that the reserved reaction to *Modern Life Is Rubbish* merely fuelled their resolve: "We were at an all time low and I remember going to the record company and saying "You've just got to let us do it, in six months' time you'll be signing bands who sound English because it's going to be what everyone wants."

• • •

Having thrown themselves against a tide of grunge with *Modern Life*, Blur now had to take their new music out on the road. They were not about to bottle out, and on a dozen album dates the stage was cluttered with all the trappings of a pantomime modern life – toasters, sofas, flying ducks, lampshades, a greasy cooker and fridge, and a TV playing local news and adverts. If U2 had their global Zooropa, this was Blur's "Shitty bedsit-ooropa". A warm up date for the national tour at Washington Heights in Reading was warmly received and things got steadily better. The band came on to the bizarre fairground reject 'Intermission' which got proceedings off to a suitably frantic start. The new album material was delivered as full-on punk for this tour, and Damon's demented stage antics were revitalised to schizoid heights. The band's first two singles were still here, but this was a respectful, duty bound nod to posterity. As ever, Blur's live set was far more weighty and fierce than on record. There was more here to remind people of '76 than '67. The gigs were all sold out, and an extra date had to be added at London's Astoria.

After initial sales peaked at only 30,000, *Modern Life* continued to sell gradually over the summer, while the tour and some festival dates kept the momentum going. Unfortunately, the response in Europe was pretty poor. Despite covering all the corners of the Continent, including a scary excursion aboard a decrepit Aeroflot charter plane to the Soviet state of Estonia, Blur's new angle didn't seem to click, and record sales were disappointingly low.

Undeterred, Blur reinforced their creative renaissance at the end of June with the release of another single 'Chemical World'. This track was originally intended to placate the dissatisfied American label SBK, but they rejected it and eventually put out the original demo version. SBK even tried to get Blur to re-record the entire album with *Nevermind* producer Butch Vig. With its snarling guitars and stop-start drums, it was one of the album's strongest musical tracks, possibly Graham's finest piece on that record. Far stronger musically than vocally, it was an odd choice of single perhaps, with clear references to Mott The Hoople and Madness. Damon's vocals were a little odd, vacillating between his new-found depth and his old affected squeak, but the chorus redeemed him. Many have seen this as another turning point – Blur seem to have had more turning points than a privet maze – but this is patently not so.

'Chemical World' reached No. 28 as with 'For Tomorrow', another relatively muted commercial success. Fortunately, the band's slowly building momentum did not stall.

This was largely due to the continued live renaissance. During the dark days of 1992, Blur gigs were a drunken, unsavoury mess. With the new focus came a new live energy. At the Nottingham Woolaston Park Free Festival they were excellent. At their warm up for Reading they were superb, and at the festival itself they were blinding, the highlight of the weekend for many. The Reading bill was an oddly sombre affair, with the designer rebellion of Rage Against The Machine alongside New Order, Dinosaur Jr, The The and Porno For Pyros. As Matt Johnson rather unfairly went down like a lead balloon, droves of people walked across to the second stage to see the headlining modern lifers. It was a crucial triumph, and possibly the very moment when people started taking Blur seriously again.

Damon himself sees this particular show as a triumph, as he told NME: "That was amazing. It was the first time I was ever in control of my performance. It was a lovely feeling, and I suddenly realised what we were, I discovered the key, the eclectic quality of gathering lots of different kinds of people together." This gig perhaps more than any after the album confirmed Blur's substantial transformation from baggy flop tops and would-be tour abuse casualties to seriously accomplished songwriters ploughing a unique and fertile furrow. In the space of eighteen months, Blur had grown from a fashionable band with no lyrics, musical depth or thematic manifesto to an opinionated, articulate and musically diverse new force. It had been an unlikely and intriguing re-invention, but hardly a painless one. Blur were back from the brink.

●　●　●

Whilst Modern Life continued to sell conservatively but at least persistently, Blur agreed to headline a Melody Maker sponsored tour called Sugary Tea (a line taken from 'Chemical World'). For each of the 14 nights they were supported by Salad and a local band, and as an added extra there were three public debates, with Blur appearing at an open forum to answer questions. At these discussions, in Newcastle, Coventry and Brighton, many questions centred around Blur's boot boy image, but Damon defended the band strongly, saying: "We're not crazed patriots, not at all. I'm just not ashamed of using what I've grown up with as a creative aid. Our culture's less embarrassing than America's." He also laughed at the stifling and very short-lived Riot Grrrl movement and belittled excessive political correctness. They talked of their embracing Englishness and how it had given them a new focus and direction, as well as how they had left their drunken, listless days behind. Once again Damon proved himself to be the most articulate and outspoken of the four. Blur had a media trump card in their singer.

The gigs themselves saw a stage set trimmed down from the cluttered front room of the previous tour, with only a television connected to an archaic space invaders game. The second album material and the dashings of still newer stuff (a song called 'Girls And Boys' was frequently aired during the tour), gave their set a revitalised energy and even tired older songs like 'Popscene' were suddenly reborn. Suddenly, Blur seemed to have a set bulging with pop hits, smooth ballads and pure punk stormers. At the Manchester Metropolitan University gig, Damon ended the set by saying: "We were bloody marvellous tonight", a stark contrast to his opening line at the disastrous Gimme Shelter gig of the previous summer.

To coincide with these dates, Blur released a new single 'Sunday Sunday' and a long form video, Star Shaped. The single, one from the sessions with Steve Lovell, was a damning judgement of the Americanisation of England. While a Sunday supplement nuclear family take their kids to McDonald's because the Sunday roast has been ruined, an old soldier reminisces about the good old days. The opening drums and clanging guitars are embellished by chirpy brass sections, then halfway through it all goes mental, speeding up to thrash velocity with swirling bingo organs. Dave Balfe hated this instrumental break, but Blur got their own way and it stayed – just as well, because it became a central feature of the song. Interestingly, the B-side finally aired some Seymour demos which had been around since 1989, with 'Tell Me, Tell Me', 'Long Legged' and 'Mixed Up' revealing just how far the band had come since their pyjama-clad beginnings. A second format had odd cover versions of the old music hall classics 'Let's All Go Down The Strand' and 'Daisy Bell'. Blur were now plunging head-first into their English experience, even though not everyone was convinced – yet. 'Sunday Sunday' reached No. 26 in October 1993, again not a stunning hit, but another contribution to Blur's growing momentum.

The Star Shaped video was hailed as an impressively honest account of a band slipping into genuine tour psychosis and ravaging themselves with booze and despair. It chronicled the period from mid-1991 to mid-1993 and the disastrous frame of mind they were in at the time. Among the catalogue of excess, we see Graham shooting puke out of his nose, Dave never without a can of beer and Damon vomiting on his shoes and saluting his own sick. In 85 sordid minutes, Blur go from sweet faced bowl haircuts to dishevelled yobs with drink problems. The highlight is the now-famous moment when an interviewer asks them what it was like to be in Blur in 1992 and is answered by stony silence. This was a genuine fly-on-the-tour-bus account.

Despite the squalid scenes, Blur were keen to schedule a sequel, perhaps based around proposed Australian and Japanese tours. Damon later told NME: "Rock musicians have a real fear of embarrassing themselves and that's why Star Shaped is quite unusual and interesting. It's good because it's so natural and because we don't act up to the camera. You couldn't have scripted it, that's for sure."

The same could be said for the band's continued recovery – many eyes were now on Blur as a not-so-dark-horse to revitalise English music.

# 7

## Pretty England And Me

1993 had been an encouraging year for British music. Although the slacker hegemony of grunge was still dominant, there were a few signs of resistance. Suede's much heralded début album hit No. 1 and they swept up the Mercury Music Prize as well as countless other industry media awards. Bands like The Boo Radleys, The Auteurs and Blur seemed to add to that peculiar English focus.

Interesting developments were taking place in a multi-ethnic Britain, with bands like Apache Indian, Fun-Da-Mental, Cornershop, Collapsed Lung and Trans-Global Underground all producing exciting new music. Whether the failure of these multi-ethnic bands to break into the mainstream reflected their own inability (doubtful) or the prejudicial barriers facing them in a medium dominated by white guitar bands is beyond the scope of this book. Suffice to say, Blur gigs, and Britpop shows in general, were not often graced with many ethnic faces (indeed, perhaps it should have been called Eng-Pop, as the majority of the groups were *English*). The future seemed to lay in the hands of a new guard of guitar-based white rock once more.

Blur seemed well placed in this renaissance, but Suede were still the leading contenders. *Modern Life* won few end of year polls, although Blur did scoop the *Melody Maker* Best Live Act category. Blur quietly continued to build on their recent progress. A few New Year dates in America were reasonably well received, but Damon's continued criticism of the States was never going to win him too many friends there. He lambasted Nirvana's use of an 8-track and Steve 'Mr Sparse' Albini's production ethics for their hugely anticipated follow up to *Nevermind* as "a pathetic aspiration".

Elsewhere, Blur's musical proficiency was increasingly recognised. Damon was asked to write the theme tune for a Steven Berkoff film entitled *Decadence*, which he did eagerly: "I've always wanted to go back to my theatrical roots, and it was wonderful to be asked. The producer cottoned on to what we were doing and was confident in us." Also, and much to the band's delight, George Harrison was seen on MTV saying how he felt Blur were excellent songwriters. A support slot to Siouxsie and The Banshees in Portugal at a stadium gig full of Goths was also played with consummate ease.

By early 1994, the pseudo-mod reinvention for their second album was definitely appealing to increasingly large numbers. So, when Blur re-emerged with a new single as a precursor to the new album, eyebrows were raised again at yet another image change. Gone were the turned-up Levis, Dr. Martens and sharp suits, in came the 1984 casual look, complete with Tachini shirts, Ellesse track suits, fawn corduroys (slit at the ankle of course) and coloured suede Puma trainers. To complement the new look, Blur released a single in March 1994 to launch the new campaign. The song was called 'Girls & Boys' and things would never be the same again.

Just when we were filing our Small Faces and Kinks records next to *Modern Life*, Blur sent us scurrying back for our early Eighties electro disco pop collection, rooting out our dust covered Giorgio Moroder and Sparks records. 'Girls & Boys' opened with a rinky dink riff and a robotic drum machine beat which crashed in with one of Alex's finest bass lines yet. Graham's phased guitar was quirky, piercing and oddly infectious, the keyboards were humorously mechanical and Damon's vocals were as affected as ever, camp yet yobbish. Suddenly, Blur made perfect sense.

If the music was a leap forward, the lyrics took Damon on to a plateau occupied by very few of his peers. This was an ambiguous celebration of the fuck 'n' chuck mentality of the notorious 18-30 style vacations. Lines about "battery thinkers, count their thoughts on 1, 2, 3, 4 , 5 fingers" and "du bist sehr schon, but we haven't been introduced" captured the meat market scenarios perfectly. Then there was the chorus – "girls who are boys who like boys to be girls who do boys like they're girls who do girls like they're boys". This was sheer pop genius. To complete the package, the sleeve artwork was taken from a cheap packet of condoms. Blur had released a gem of a single that suddenly catapulted them past all their contemporaries. It was unquestionably their finest and most audacious moment so far.

Backed with four new songs as well, the package entered the charts at No. 5, and secured massive radio play nationwide. All manner of broadcasting outlets found something in the single that fitted with their play lists. 'Single of the Week' awards flooded in and Blur were suddenly splashed across a multitude of magazine covers. It is easy to forget that despite all their traumas and triumphs, 'Girls & Boys' was in fact only Blur's eighth single.

By a strange twist of fate, Blur's triumph was largely over-shadowed by the tragic suicide of Kurt Cobain. While the music world was united in its grief, there was a definite sense that the old order had perhaps been irreparably damaged, and although wary of disrespectful haste, a new vanguard was clearly about to pounce.

What that new generation wasn't going to be was the clumsily christened New Wave Of New Wave. In the autumn of 1993, two *NME* journalists had listened to the likes of S*M*A*S*H, Blessed Ethel and These Animal Men and announced that here was British music's saviour: "The concept is New Wave of New Wave. The reality is a lumping together of (at times) vaguely like-minded fresh British bands with ants in their pants and vocabularies laced with shrapnel." The two key players, S*M*A*S*H and These Animal Men, were lyrically astute and articulate in their clarion call to rebellion, and their energetic and vibrant live shows seemed initially to offer the injection that was so needed.

Then in the New Year of 1994, the New Wave Of New Wave went overground with magazine covers and packed gigs, and a whole host of bands were included, including Done Lying Down, Action Painting and even Elastica. The movement was as important sartorially as it was for the rather one dimensional, speed-fuelled music, which harped back to The Jam and The Clash, but the NWONW's days were numbered. When Blur released 'Girls & Boys' they effectively killed NWONW. First baggy, then grunge, now this.

By the end of 1994, many of the NWONW bands had split and barely any long term success was achieved – in retrospect, the movement had no more cultural significance than shoe-gazing. To add insult to injury, Damon was quite happy to claim that 'Popscene' had actually invented NWONW anyway (Blur briefly considered re-releasing the single as a NWONW cash in). Even Dave, who was used to Damon's espousing by now, was uncomfortable with this one: "Oh no, I think we're going to claim we invented everything again."

The release of *Parklife* rendered all this discussion instantly irrelevant. The rest of 1994 was spent in creating new media superlatives for an album immediately recognised as a landmark British record. Things had not augured so well at the album launch party. Having spent much of their careers ligging at everyone else's expense, it was nice to see the compliment returned, with the likes of Pop Will Eat Itself, Sleeper, Elastica, Pet Shop Boys, Carter, Lush, The Cranberries, Jesus Jones, Eddie Izzard and Eddie Tenpole Tudor all turning up to an East End dog track. A riotous evening was had by all, and everything went like clockwork, until the Blur sponsored 'Parklife Stakes', when it all went hilariously wrong. One dog got stuck in the trap, then shortly after the hare became dislodged and the

remaining dogs tried to rip it, and then themselves, to pieces. Pandemonium ensued and the race was declared void - the gold presentation box of *Parklife* and a £90 first prize remained uncollected. Damon was typically philosophical when he told the media: "Slow start, always led, strong finish."

'Girls & Boys' had raised the stakes considerably for Blur and many wondered if they could reproduce that quality across a whole album. *Parklife* silenced all doubters, and the cynics who had dogged Blur since their inception (at times justifiably so) slinked off into the background. Much of the groundwork had been done with *Modern Life* and indeed without that record there would have been no *Parklife*, but it was the latter that struck gold. This all-conquering album asserted itself as the year's best record, and perhaps the album of the decade.

It was recorded at Maison Rouge between November 1993 and January 1994, with 'To The End' being completed at RAK studios in St John's Wood. Stephen Street was at the controls and Blur again worked with customary speed. This being their second album in twelve months, Blur were clearly taking the Leiber & Stoller work ethic last seen with Morrissey and Marr to their hearts. They arrived at 11am each morning and worked solidly through until 9 or 10pm, taking only one break in the afternoon for tea.

Progress was quick – after all, songs like 'Parklife' and 'Girls & Boys' had been played in the Blur live set for *Modern Life*, so by now much of the material was well understood by the band. Very soon they had 20 tracks to choose from. Once again, a vast array of instrumentation was used, ranging from Hammonds, a Moog, harpsichord, melodica, vibraphone, various percussion, and even clarinet and saxophone, courtesy of Graham. The combination offered a sonic variety unchallenged by anyone. The array of styles was enormous, and tied in with what Hildreth had spotted in a younger Damon's tastes. The record was full of the last 30 years of pop – splashes of electro pop on 'Girls & Boys', punk rock for 'Bank Holiday', Gary Numan in 'Trouble In The Message Centre', while The Kinks, The Small Faces, Buzzcocks, Madness and The Jam gate-crash all over the record. It swept effortlessly from punk rock to ballads. Clanging sing-alongs sat uncomfortably next to robotic instrumentals and lush, string-laden epics. The Germanic 'oompah' of 'Debt Collector' is sandwiched between the seemingly incompatible sugary sweet vocals of 'Badhead' and the quirky robotic mayhem of 'Far Out'. Elsewhere, the pure pop of 'End Of A Century' is followed by the punk rock blast of 'Bank Holiday'. This kaleidoscopic range of styles could have clattered together in one unholy mess, but somehow Blur pulled it off, with the variety adding to their achievement, rather than cluttering it up.

Thematically, *Parklife* introduced oddball characters and weird scenarios that had been fermenting in Damon's head for months. Whereas some bands looked to drugs and tour misbehaviour in a desperate attempt to shock, Blur looked inward at the sexually and socially deviant lives of the British population. 'Tracy Jacks' was a golf playing civil servant transvestite while the barrow boy chant of 'Parklife' saw the actor Phil Daniels, who starred in *Quadrophenia*, filling the shoes of a potty park-keeper, whiling away his hours watching pigeons shag, and laughing at flabby suited men avoiding the red-faced joggers on the grass. A series of superb couplets told tales of grandma's dentures, barbecues, pizzas and Snickers bars on 'Bank Holiday', perhaps the sequel to 'Sunday Sunday'. Damon's anti-Americanism reared its head again for 'Magic America' which talked of "buildings in the sky and the air is sugar free", despising the shopping malls and cable TV culture. He even featured the Shipping Forecast, in the sad and dreamy trip around Britain's shores for what is now seen as one of Blur's greatest songs, 'This Is A Low'. This penultimate track was a dark and introspective near-finale, bulging with emotion. The two instrumental tracks 'Debt Collector' and 'Lot 105', along with 'Clover Over Dover' (noted in the sleeve as "Theme From An Imaginary Film") gave the album a cinematic quality.

Like *Modern Life*, the album reflected something of Blur's past, but unlike its predecessor it was far more wide-reaching in scope, exploiting their earlier themes with far more depth. Damon warned people of this when he said to *NME*: "This album is in a lot of ways a massive departure from the last one. If people are scared of that then there's not much I can do about it."

Damon was not holding these people up as outcasts or weirdoes, there was a genuine affection – he told *Puncture* he empathised with them: "I've always liked the idea that everybody is capable of deviant behaviour, however private. I've never been spiteful or angry about the characters – their malevolence is just comical. They're all doing peculiar things in small ways, not making a big fuss about it."

Damon later revealed that the rivalry with Suede, and his belief that they had stolen some of his ideas, had been a major motivation during the writing of this album. Even so, Suede's focus tended to be more romanticised, more ambient drama, whereas Blur's was a very real, very gritty London of false teeth and fly-overs. "I use London for a metaphor for almost every situation I'm in," Damon told *NME*. "I can't help it. I never think of London as just one person, there's so many different elements to it. It's not one girlfriend, it's twenty." Damon also denied in the *NME* that this was another record in danger of getting lost in fascist rhetoric, saying all his characters were actually fed up and trying to escape England: "The English are so mean-spirited, and I am ashamed, but that's us isn't it? I suppose our songs are just telling each other how crap we are. All my songs criticise this country."

The third person narrative style enabled Damon to recount all the lurid stories of his cast with superb detail. Back in the autumn of 1991, Damon had once been asked "what do you stand for?" to which he answered "so we don't have to keep lying down." It is sometimes hard to believe that this was the same lyricist as on *Parklife*.

Much of what the media said was very accurate. The central theory was that Blur were the next in line of a long heritage of English pop, going back to the groups of the Sixties, in particular The Small Faces and The Kinks, through bands like Buzzcocks, The Jam and Madness, and on to the electro pop of Gary Numan. Albums such as The Kinks' *The Village Green Preservation Society* were cited

as similar examples of narrative records with revealing vignettes of English life and insights behind the net curtains. At the time of *Parklife*, such lyrical tale-telling was still largely unfashionable, so it was a brave reference point for Blur (it was not entirely new, though – Blur admitted many of these influences way back on *Leisure*).

There was also a 'quaint' nature to some tracks, like 'Trouble In The Message Centre' that again fitted in with this British heritage. There were lyrical similarities to Ray Davies of The Kinks, as well as more unusual analogies for 'Tracy Jacks', a sexual misfit possibly descended from Pink Floyd's 'Arnold Layne'. Damon's vocal delivery especially tied him to The Small Faces, and Graham's guitar linked back to craftsmen like Johnny Marr. Blur readily admitted their influences, and openly revered many of the bands they were now being compared to. The point to remember is that the result was always greater, or rather *different* to the sum of its parts. Nothing wasted, only reproduced.

● ● ●

Beyond the British pop, there was a second – and largely ignored – musical strain echoing around *Parklife*. This was the music hall heritage which directly inspired tracks like 'The Debt Collector' and 'Lot 105', and indirectly influenced much of Blur's very essence. Various British bands had played around with early music hall and vaudeville, most notably The Beatles whose 'Being For The Benefit Of Mr Kite' from the *Sgt. Pepper* album is perhaps the best known example. Herman's Hermits enjoyed success with music hall pastiches (Trevor Peacock's 'Mrs Brown, You've Got A Lovely Daughter') as well as actual music hall ('I'm Henry The Eighth I Am'). Their front man Peter Noone was a pretty faced drama student whose theatrical style and cute, gap-toothed smile reaped rich rewards for the band.

Music hall as an entertainment tradition was largely fading by the late Forties, having enjoyed a heyday in the late Victorian era through to the Twenties. During the Fifties and Sixties it was increasingly replaced by variety shows, with the likes of Danny Kaye and other Americans headlining venues like The London Palladium and Victoria Palace. Many of the original British music hall stars, including the great Marie Lloyd, had a performance style peculiar to British music hall tradition known as 'audience address' which meant singing *to* the crowd, rather than *at* it. This was most obvious on Lloyd's song "The Boy I Love Is Up In The Gallery" from the turn of the century, but the style shone through on many of her songs, including the well known 'My Old Man Said Follow The Van'.

Damon Albarn brings a dramatic quality to Blur shows, and that theatricality is evident on their records. In the case of *Parklife*, it is easy to imagine Damon singing 'To The End' to an actual member of the stalls. He told *The Face*: "There is a lot of acting in me. The characters I create exist

for me, and I have to be them for the three minutes I am singing it." On *Parklife*, there are direct music hall spin-offs, but there are also more subtle examples, such as the title track which employs a humour and ultra-reality that was a core element of this style of music.

There has been a long tradition of music hall and musical writers working in the pop vein, and Damon was inverting that age-old trend. Just as Lionel Bart had followed the legendary *Oliver* with pop songs for Tommy Steele, so Damon was following very modern pop songs such as 'Bank Holiday' with throw-backs such as 'Debt Collector'. Damon has made it clear he sees himself very much in this vein: "I am part of a tradition. I am part of a music hall-clown-entertainer tradition that's been in this country since the turn of the century. It's a theatrical tradition which if you come from this country you lean into. It's like pantomime, we've all been to those at Christmas, so it's in our blood. I used to love going to pantomime and always feel the need to entertain."

Another influence is the radical theatre of Joan Littlewood, who worked at The Theatre Royal Stratford East. Damon's mother worked there while pregnant with Damon, and one of Littlewood's greatest productions was *Oh, What A Lovely War,* which was one of the key musicals in which Damon participated at Stanway Comprehensive. But it goes deeper than that. Littlewood, along with partner Gerry Raffles, pretty much single-handedly changed the face of British music theatre in the late Fifties, fighting off the influx of American actors, and casting home-grown innovators instead. There is a parallel in what Littlewood achieved here with *Parklife*'s achievements – the fourth Blur album heralded a new era of British music, when the crown of pop was snatched away from visiting American bands. Similarly, Littlewood took alternative theatre which pre-dated the fringe circuit and invaded the West End mainstream. Forty years later and Blur were leaving the pages of *NME* to appear on the covers of nationwide tabloids, at huge venues and on arena tours, with the year's most critically acclaimed album under their belts.

One of the hardiest followers of the Littlewood school of thought was East 15, where Damon attended drama school in his late teens. Damon always refers back to this acting background and clearly enjoys applying these skills on stage with Blur. Simply Red would have gone to RADA, Damon went to East 15, the angry young man's drama school. It was Tom Courtenay taking on Gielgud. Blur outselling Wet Wet Wet. Both were new waves in their own right.

The other key link is Brecht-Weill who also pre-date Sixties pop. Having participated in *Die Drei Groschen Oper* with its hit song 'Mack The Knife' at East 15, Damon was aware at an early stage of the oddities and almost atonal appeal of some of Weill's music. He was also a fan of Brecht's radical playwriting and bits of both can be seen in Blur's work. Most obvious is the influence of Weill, whose odd chromaticisms and nuances are mirrored in the way

Brecht

Weill

Blur take the popular form and twist it, especially on songs like 'Debt Collector', which has remarkable similarities to the stylistic brashness of *Die Drei Groschen Oper*. While Blur are nowhere near as political as Brecht, the fresh subject matter and unique characters were similar features.

Pushing the connection still further, there is an esoteric similarity between Blur's open attitude to their reverential use of pop's past and Brecht's infamous 'Theatre of Alienation'. This was best seen during the work of The Berliner Ensemble (again something that Damon had worked with in his teens), where the cast abandoned all traditional attempts to suspend audience belief – they walked on stage without a curtain, did not hide the lights or have complex scenery, and even introduced themselves as actors who were about to perform a play. Now, obviously Blur don't do this live, but creating a pastiche that is greater than the sum of its parts is more than apparent on *Parklife*. Indeed, Blur's honest admissions about plundering the past were first expressed in interviews for *Modern Life*. They are both saying "we know you know, but look and listen, it is still something new and special."

One final parallel is with Damon and Kurt Weill's writing prowess. Weill is still seen today as a classical composer in his own right, and yet he also went on to write popular songs ('September Song', covered by Lou Reed, 'Alabama Song', covered by both David Bowie and The Doors, and 'Mack The Knife', covered by everybody), folk opera ('Down In The Valley') and Broadway musicals ('Knickerbocker Holiday' and ('One Touch Of Venus'). Similarly, Damon has started off writing linear pop of the day ('There's No Other Way'), but has also written film themes ('Decadence' and a track for *Trainspotting* entitled 'Closet Romantic'; Blur also contributed 'Sing' to the soundtrack), and has had his work arranged for orchestra. Even the Steven Berkoff connection is also relevant – Berkoff comes very much from the school of Brecht and Weill, and is famed for his highly physical performances – something Damon was also renowned for in Blur's early days.

Blur's many influences dispel the critical perception that the band are a throwback to the Sixties. "I can't agree we are a Sixties band," says Damon. "I think we are a very Nineties band, the only Nineties band around. If you're going to analyse a set of individuals and their music, you've got to look further than what you see on the record. Journalists always try to look further without knowing enough."

He has even given hints about where to look, as he suggested in the infamous 'Empire Under Siege' article: "We have such a rich musical heritage, and it doesn't just start with rock'n'roll, it goes back to the post-war period of Joan Littlewood and Lionel Bart, and before that to Music Hall."

Whatever your view of *Parklife*, it was undeniably a classic album. In a pop world where CD's have enabled listeners to flit effortlessly from track to track, here was an album that demanded playing all the way through, time and time again. Among all the protracted discussions and theories that surrounded the year's most celebrated album, just one sentence in the *NME* summed it all up perfectly: "It is easy to forget that albums can be this fabulous".

# 8

## Jubilee

**Vintage 1994, very fruity**

The musical quality of *Parklife* translated into a colossal commercial success. Much to the band's amazement, it outsold Pink Floyd's chart topping *The Division Bell* by three to one and entered the charts straight at No. 1. *Parklife* went on to stay in the Top 20 for 90 weeks and sell over 1.8 million copies. It captured the very Zeitgeist of the moment like no other album of the Nineties, and the run of achievements seemed endless. *Parklife* was nominated for the prestigious Mercury Music Award from a list of 130 acts, along with excellent records by The Prodigy, Therapy?, Paul Weller and Pulp. Blur were pre-match favourites at 2-1 to take the award that Suede had won the year before, but they were all beaten to the post by M People's soulless pop, apparently seizing the crown from Pulp's *His 'n' Hers* by just one vote.

*Select* hailed Blur as 'The Best British Band Since The Smiths' claiming that *Parklife* was the guitar pop album by which all other records of the next decade would be judged. Damon even achieved his life-long ambition of appearing on the BBC Radio 4 chat show *Loose Ends* with Ned Sherrin. With mass coverage in the music press, the tabloids, the teen mags and the broadsheets, Blur had now successfully straddled the often impossible gap between critical acclaim and mass commercial success

The extent to which Blur had crossed over into the mainstream only became fully apparent during the tour to promote *Parklife*. Starting in May 1994, the 16 dates took in relatively small venues, considering that Blur were now arguably the biggest young band in the country, with Nottingham's Rock City as the opener. As the tour progressed, the success of *Parklife* increased, so that by the last date Blur were being greeted as conquering heroes.

**"Please give a hand for... Jesus"**

Damon in particular was being treated like some kind of pop messiah. At one show in Wolverhampton he crowd surfed and lost his shoe, then clambered back on stage and said "I need my shoe back, I'm not Jesus you know" at which point the crowd began chanting "Je-sus, Je-sus". This routine

became a regular feature of Blur gigs, and on this tour alone Damon lost six pairs of shoes. The popular appeal of *Parklife* was reinforced by the sing-along nature of most of these Blur gigs – the audience participation was immense, especially on the title track.

Blur were assisted on these dates by Cara Tivey on keyboards who filled out the musical textures of the set when Damon was too preoccupied with being Jesus. He was highly theatrical now, drawing on his drama background to play the roles of his characters on stage, colourfully animating the songs one minute, then plunging head first into a sea of hands the next. His oft-maligned Mockney accent was getting sharper and sharper, and he hammed it up, drawing in the swooning girls and admiring lads.

Alongside Damon's greater stage dramatics, Dave's drumming was noticeably more precise. Having drunk like a fish on tour in the past, he had now gone tee-total. "Mentally I got quite ill," he told *NME*. "I started to get very paranoid, I was always a miserable drunk and when I got pissed it started to affect me mentally." One morning after a huge binge with Siouxsie and The Banshees at a stadium gig in Portugal, Dave decided that enough was enough, and stopped there and then. He had recently married and felt it was no longer acceptable to survive on a purely liquid diet. Since then, Dave has been regularly taunted by the band for his sobriety. He said to *Melody Maker*: "I miss things like going down the pub. Do I miss the oblivion? Well, I can't say I do because I could never remember anything. The reason I stopped had a lot to do with waking up with a hangover every day for three years."

Graham meanwhile seemed to vacillate between disinterested and bored on stage. The shyest member of Blur, his demeanour was borne of studiously playing his ever-more complex guitar lines, mastering his effects and being too scared to look up. Alex, on the other hand was not so shy. With an ever-present fag hanging out of the corner of his mouth and his lanky body curling round the bass, he was suave and smouldering.

Backstage, the band were plagued by press and groupies, but still managed to enjoy themselves. Lager was the drink of their choice – this was still Essex man on tour, playing mainstream songs about middle and working-class people, eulogising in interviews about their manifesto and christening themselves, in Damon's words, "mythical lager eaters". Blur were quick to deny any suggestion of drug use however, at least Damon was, as he told *Melody Maker*: "A lot of people I know take too many drugs. It messes with their emotions and in their quietest darkest hours makes them very unhappy. It certainly has nothing to do with creativity."

With *Parklife* sales showing no sign of slowing down, the Blur steamroller continued. At the Glastonbury Festival, the nation's current favourites found themselves only on the second stage (and not even headlining that), as the show had been booked before *Parklife* was released. They played alongside Radiohead, Inspiral Carpets and before headliners Spiritualized. Damon took to the stage in Druids' robes while Graham, for some reason, performed in full combat gear, complete with regulation helmet. Blur were in esteemed company, with Peter Gabriel, Björk, Orbital, Rage Against The Machine, Paul Weller and Elvis Costello also playing the festival, but as with Reading the previous year they took the honours.

The story was not so rosy in Europe during an extensive tour which took in most of the Continent and included many summer festivals. *Parklife* was the most British album for years, and despite Europe being an open market the cultural divide has yet to be bridged. The sheer complete Englishness of people like Tracy Jacks and Blur's comic park-keeper were largely lost on Continental audiences, and much of the media still had Blur down as another Jesus Jones. Shows were well attended and reasonably well received, but there was nowhere near the impact seen back at home. The only other downside to this series of live dates was when Alex returned home after a gig in Shepherd's Bush and found he'd been burgled. In typically nonchalant fashion, he said he didn't mind because he never gave money to beggars!

● ● ●

It was typically perverse of Blur to release 'To The End' as the second single from *Parklife*. The lush string-soaked ballad could have easily been a John Barry film theme. With its Anglo-French lyrics and a rich campness throughout, this was another turning point for Blur which elevated their writing in the eyes of contemporaries and record-buying public alike. It reached No. 16 in the charts in June, but more importantly attracted a whole new audience to the band. Whereas 'Girls & Boys' had scooped up thousands of new younger pop fans, this elegant ballad won over countless older listeners, a fact confirmed by the variety of age groups attending Blur gigs after this single. Blur also found time to appear at the *NME* film festival entitled 'Punk Before And Beyond', where *Star Shaped* was shown.

Blur returned to the pop stakes in early September with 'Parklife', the third single from the album and the best song ever about pigeons. Phil Daniels' cameo performance was perfect for the nutty central character, and made Damon's live version seem rather tame. This appearance mirrored Stanley Unwin's barmy showing on The Small Faces *Ogden's Nut Gone Flake*. Daniels was in many ways a theatrical parallel to Blur. He had starred as Jimmy, the schizophrenic Mod in *Quadrophenia*, the film based on The Who's 1973 double album, which was made at the height of the late Seventies Mod revival. Jimmy entered Mod mythology by driving his scooter over the white cliffs of Dover, an act mirrored in Blur's 'Clover Over Dover'. Daniels had also appeared in several Mike Leigh films including *Meantime*, a perennial favourite of Damon and Graham's. Furthermore, Daniels had always expressed a distaste for Hollywood and American culture, and while many of his contemporaries moved across the water to sunnier and more glamorous climes, he stayed firmly put in England.

'Parklife' was, of course, a madcap choice for a single, but a considerable commercial success nonetheless, reaching No. 10. In keeping with Blur's prolific approach, there were two new instrumental tracks included in the package,

'Supa Shoppa' and 'Beard' as well as a much sought after French version of 'To The End'. This had been recorded with Françoise Hardy, the Parisian chanteuse.

This release preceded Blur's two biggest ever headline gigs in Britain, at the Aston Villa Leisure Centre on October 5 and the cavernous Alexandra Palace two days later. Their only other planned date in the autumn was a headline slot at Glasgow's 'T In The Park', along with Manic Street Preachers and D:Ream. Preparation came in the form of a warm-up date at Cambridge Corn Exchange – a sizeable gig for many bands but now merely a small quickie for Blur. The Aston Villa gig sold out in hours, and Radio 1 broadcast the performance live as part of their 'Octoberfest' season of shows which also featured Suede and Sinéad O'Connor. The Alexandra Palace gig had been announced back in early August, the same week that *Parklife* achieved gold album sales of over 100,000. Blur were worried about their ability to sell enough tickets – after all, the hangar-like venue hadn't heard a guitar played in anger since The Stone Roses in 1989. Yet within three days of the show being announced they'd had enough enquiries to fill Alexandra Palace five times.

1994 was a year of superlatives for Blur, and their Midas touch seemed endemic. If any single moment encapsulated everything about their achievement, all that they stood for and all that they had fought against, it was this triumphant Ally Pally gig. On an impressive bill were an infant Supergrass (one of Damon's favourite bands), Corduroy and the voyeuristic Pulp, one of the few bands who shared Damon's liking for behind-the-net-curtains Britain, and perhaps the only act capable of supporting Blur with any credibility at this show. For a mere £2.40 extra, fans could buy Blur Rover tickets, which included transport back to Trafalgar Square after the gig.

On the night, proceedings began early at 6.45pm, with Supergrass showing signs of the talent that would send them supernova in the spring of 1995. Corduroy were largely forgettable, but Pulp certainly weren't and unlikely sex god Jarvis Cocker charmed everyone with his limp-wristed foppery and unique 'epileptic coat hanger in a suit' style of dancing. During the intermission, ladies sold ice creams and handed out bingo tickets. The top prize was "A Night Out With Blur." Shortly after, a bingo caller came on and started reading out the numbers, and gradually every single person in the hall began crossing off all the numbers. When the last number was called out, 7,000 people had a full house and Blur walked on stage to a Palace full of winners.

The stage set was a monument to Blur's peculiar domestic fascinations with huge red lampshades swamping the stage (Blur lost money on this gig because of the operation costs). Launching off with 'Tracy Jacks' followed by a soaring rendition of 'Popscene', everything clicked - the stage set, the brass sections, the band's musical performance, and especially the Phil Daniels rendition of 'Parklife' which sent the audience nuclear. Neither the raw egg that hit Damon nor the lack of new material other than 'Mr Robinson's Quango' seemed to matter. Towards the end of the set, Damon hushed the crowd and thanked them with heartfelt and genuine gratitude for the way they had treated Blur in 1994. All the arrogant and overtly ambitious claims that he had spewed out in interviews over the years made perfect sense. Fortunately, for those unable to get in, the band released a long form video of the gig in February 1995 entitled 'Show Time'. The artwork was typical Blur, with an old-school painted clown pronouncing "Re-live the thrill of it all – Family entertainment up the Ally Pally".

Simon Exton's 'A' Level
re-arrangement of 'Parklife'

The band's success was not universal however. The reception in the USA was only luke-warm, reinforcing the gulf between what Blur represented and what the American audience wanted to hear. Such was the absolute failure of *Modern Life Is Rubbish* in America that most people thought *Parklife* was the follow-up to *Leisure.* There was pressure on Blur to succeed Stateside – after all, they had pretty much conquered the home market now, so it was the next logical step. Blur themselves did not see it this way, and chose to visit only nine cities including Los Angeles, Boston, Chicago, and San Francisco, supported by Pulp on all dates. They travelled by plane, and everything was done to avoid a repeat of the débâcle of their last US tour. The impact of *Parklife* was therefore inevitably limited, but that was as much to do with the music and subject matter as the size of the tour. Suffice to say, the dates sold out well in advance, albeit in venues of between 1,000-1,500 capacity. Those that did attend were fanatical, and the band were highly amused to see small collections of Mods on Lambrettas outside each gig.

Blur rounded off the year with the release in November of the fourth single from *Parklife,* the jaunty pop of 'End Of A Century'. The record was perhaps most notable for the duo of appalling B-sides written by Alex and Graham. Graham's 'Red Necks' was a laughable comic Country & Western track which accompanied the single, whilst other formats carried Alex's fantastically titled 'Alex's Song'. This suggested that 'Far Out', written by Alex for *Parklife*, might well be a one-off, and confirmed Damon's claim that... "Alex only writes a song every two years and they're all about planets." The inferior musical package mattered little – by now the momentum surrounding Blur almost guaranteed them hits, so the single reached No. 19. They had notched up another hit, and it made their travels around an unconvinced Europe at this time a little more comfortable.

There was no let up for Blur right until Christmas. Damon fronted *Top Of The Pops* and then they appeared on *Later With Jools Holland,* alongside Stevie Winwood and Ruby Turner. However, the best event of this Yuletide period was definitely the band's secret gig at Colchester Sixth Form College on December 16. Considering they had just been on a world tour taking in Japan, Scandinavia, Europe and America, Colchester was hardly the next logical port of call. Nigel Hildreth wanted to raise funds for an orphanage in India, so he called Damon's father Keith and asked if his former pupil would mind making a personal appearance. Much to his amazement, Damon said that rather than just turn up and sign autographs, he would much rather play a gig at the College, which had now relocated to a site on North Hill in the town centre, just up from the Army Recruitment centre. Furthermore, Damon said he wanted Hildreth's class to arrange six Blur songs and accompany them on stage with their own 17-piece school orchestra.

Hildreth takes up the story: "We had a major security problem on our hands now, because Blur were massive and our gym is hardly the size of Alexandra Palace. So we finalised details and gave the students the sheet music, and then on the morning of the gig, I was just talking to the class about some homework and I said 'Oh, by the way, Blur are coming in tonight to play a gig in the gym'.

"Damon had said the charity side appealed to him, but also the fact that it was so intimate – they seemed uncomfortable with the big arenas they were now playing. Needless to say, there were outsiders absolutely frantic to get in, but it was a strictly students-only performance, that was the whole point. All the engineers and record company people were fantastic, and during the day they all gave their time for free – Blur seem to have an excellent crew and group of friends around them. I was in London for a boring meeting that afternoon, and I was late getting to the train station to get back to Colchester, so I just dived on the first carriage as it pulled away and there was this big cry of "Heh! Mr. Hildreth, over here!" I looked up and Blur were sitting there. I went over and had a chat but when the conductor came I had to go to the second class compartment."

Hildreth and Damon worked on the musical arrangements right up to the last minute, and they also talked about the school days they had shared. Damon made it quite clear he was grateful to Hildreth's open attitude, and told *Kaleidoscope*: "He gave me and Graham a real confidence about doing lots of things, neither of us are incredibly proficient, he gave us that confidence to busk it really." He also privately thanked him for shouting at him all those times his mind had wandered!

The new school site was built after a disgruntled ex-teacher burnt the old building down, an act that could have easily slotted into Blur's suburban world. Local papers had enjoyed a hate/hate relationship with Blur ever since Damon's early criticisms of the town. He once remarked: "There's an unwritten law in Colchester that says you can talk about it but never achieve it." They had returned the insult with negative coverage, which now backfired on them as they were all banned from the show, although the gig still made the front page of the *Colchester Evening Gazette* – fame at last. When the 5pm showtime arrived, Damon walked on to a stage covered in tinsel and fairy lights and said "Hello, thanks for coming, nice to be back" and launched into 'End Of A Century', at which point the 400 strong audience went into mass hysteria. Among the songs arranged by the students were 'Parklife', 'Tracy Jacks', 'To The End', 'End Of A Century', 'Debt Collector' (Simon Exton, the student who had re-arranged 'Parklife' later submitted the piece for his 'A' level music course). There was some discussion about releasing tracks from the show with the orchestra, but the recording quality wasn't suitable. To cap it all, they raised £3,000 for the charity fund.

After the gig, they all piled into the nearest pub and later Damon and Hildreth visited Colchester Arts Centre, the scene of one of Damon's earliest gigs all those years ago. Perhaps the best part of the night was when Alex missed his bass cue for 'Girls & Boys', whereupon Damon immediately stopped the song. "No! no! no!," he said. "You've missed it. Now, if you'd been taught by Mr. Hildreth, you wouldn't have done that. You wouldn't have dared!"

Not for the first time, Mr. Hildreth points Damon and Graham in the right direction

Colchester 6th Form College, secret gig, December 1994

SHAN
0734 811244

# 9

## London Loves

By the time of Blur's pre-Christmas secret gig, Britain was gripped by the phenomenon known as Britpop. 'Britpop' is a media fiction, a movement christened by outsiders and not by the bands deemed to be involved. Labels of convenience have littered music writing since the term 'Merseybeat' was coined to describe The Beatles and their contemporaries from Liverpool, and all subsequent attempts to pigeon-hole bands have suffered from the same journalistic malaise.

In 1994, there was an inspired renaissance in British pop music that saw a whole slew of new native bands enjoy various degrees of success. With the rise of American slacker-driven grunge culture, British music had been largely ignored during the early Nineties, ever since the demise of Madchester. Since American grunge was largely album-based, the UK singles charts were swamped with one hit wonders, cover versions, novelty songs and old timers. Britpop changed all this.

Many factors combined to create Britpop. Suede's arrival in 1992 was a key catalyst, and their highly stylised, romantic London dramas, and Brett's peculiar camp Englishness, led the way. Pat Gilbert of *Record Collector* is a fan of Britpop and he believes Suede were essential to its inception: "Britpop's genesis has its roots in Suede, who were the first post-indie band who refused to be mulling and wantonly middle class, they didn't want to recreate three minute perfect pop songs in the line of the Velvets and The Byrds and they came along with a bit of swagger. Suede were definitely the first time in years that English bands had reclaimed some sense of occasion about what they were doing, and people started looking back at British bands rather than all that American stuff. Suede started all that."

*Modern Life* was Blur's first quintessentially English album and many of their British ideas pre-dated Suede, including – crucially – their 'our culture is under siege' philosophy. Suede's success and commercial exposure gave their ideas recognition. In April of 1993, *Select* magazine ran a feature not so subtly titled "Yanks Go Home" which featured a whole list of English style bands. With Suede on the cover, there were also articles on Pulp, St. Etienne, Denim and The Auteurs. Notably, Blur didn't even get a mention, even though advance copies of the first of their English trilogy of albums were already in circulation in the industry.

The piece carried the tongue-in-cheek line: "Who do you think you are kidding Mr. Cobain? Enough is enough! We don't want plaid. We want crimplene, glamour, wit and irony. If 1992 was the American year then it's time to bring on the Home Guard." Many consider grunge to have encapsulated a cultural low that coincided with and reflected economic depression; with the recession fading a new optimism sprang up which brought the resurgence of more buoyant British bands.

The Home Guard grew during 1993. *Modern Life* was complemented by Suede's eponymously titled award winning

Pulp, The Common People

Suede, Britpop's genesis?

Supergrass, Alright

début album. The rejuvenation of the festivals, kick-started by memorable performances by Nirvana and Pearl Jam, accelerated with stunning live shows by Blur and Suede, and also by The Boo Radleys and veteran British pioneers New Order. Nirvana's *Nevermind* follow up *In Utero* silenced some of the doubters for a while, but with designer grunge now prancing along the catwalks and grunge-by-numbers advertising American jeans, the voices of dissent grew.

1994 was when it all exploded. Gilbert believes that Britpop was jump-started by the energetic emergence of New Wave of New Wave at the tail end of 1993: "The NWONW was important in the sense that it kick-started an interest in really live energetic bands. Crucially, some of its reference points were very English, the Grange Hill 1978 schoolboy look, Adidas trainers and tops, short spiky hair, The Clash and The Sex Pistols. Perhaps it was more important sartorially than musically, in helping to define what Britpop was going to be."

Once Blur's *Parklife* pushed the speed-fuelled NWONW aside, the flood gates of Britpop opened, and the death of Kurt Cobain acted as a tragic finale to the grunge era. Throughout 1994, streams of new bands came through, and with the mainstream media picking up on Britpop, the resurgence of British music was astounding. In the next eighteen months, Pulp finally broke their fourteen year duck and produced a sexually subversive, comical masterpiece in their first major label album *His 'n' Hers*. Elastica broke away from their suffocating early NWONW status to release a volley of classic singles, stating the case for female writers, as did the more lightweight Sleeper. The Auteurs more sombre style had somewhat underachieved, but Oxford's Radiohead filled the void with an unusual début album which was soon followed by *The Bends*, universally recognised as one of the great albums of the Nineties.

In direct contrast to the saintly patience of Pulp came Supergrass, formed early in 1994, whose lively début album *I Should Coco* hit No. 1 within eighteen months of the band's formation. Their hit single 'Alright', with its infectious chorus, acted as a manifesto for Britpop fans. The ranks were also swelled by the likes of Shed Seven, Portishead, The Bluetones, Marion, Powder, Dodgy and the album chart topping Boo Radleys. There was also the ultimate derivative Britpop band Menswear, who appeared on *Top Of The Pops* before their first single was even released. Ironically, Suede experienced a bad year in 1994 with the loss of guitarist and key songwriter Bernard Butler, but with the arrival of Richard Oakes as a replacement and the release of their under-rated second album *Dog Man Star*, Suede returned from the brink. Blur at Alexandra Palace, Suede's début album, Supergrass on *Top Of The Pops* and Jarvis on *Pop Quiz* were all great Britpop moments.

Mod also underwent something of a revival, with Modfather Paul Weller enjoying renewed success after a disappointing start to his solo career, and there was renewed interest in The Small Faces – Britain's original mod band – as a result of retrospective releases and a new biography. The mod leanings that Blur showed on the second album had been shaken off, but many still tagged them as part of the new movement.

Britpop caused or coincided with ripples in other areas of the British music industry. *Top of the Pops* had a new producer, Ric Blaxill, who rejuvenated its tired format. Blur, Elastica and Pulp have all been guest presenters and scores of Britpop style bands have graced the show. Blaxill's first gig was Steve Harley at Crystal Palace in 1973 and his passion for British music remains undimmed. "My basic philosophy is that the programme is called *Top Of The Pops* and that is what it should represent, genuinely good music," he says. "Fortunately, the BBC gave me a large degree of editorial freedom to go with the bands that I wanted. I think it should feature the obvious stars, but there are also bands who maybe haven't got a huge record deal, maybe haven't got an album, maybe not even a single, who should be seen and heard. The way the programme was run before meant that each week only about six or seven record companies would be at the meeting; now I will sometimes have maybe 25 or 30 people competing for nine slots, because all manner of bands know that the door is open for them. Blur's contributions are always excellent, they know how it all works and they are a very bright band, they play up to it. Their spirit and attitude is very open, bands like that are superb for the programme."

Record sales rocketed in the UK by 14% on the previous year, so that total sales reached an all-time high of £1.5 billion. Live shows became more popular, and 14-year-olds began switching off their Nintendos and forming bands. Pat Gilbert is in no doubt that Britpop has already made a significant contribution to British musical history: "In twenty years time people will look back at 1994 and the two years after it as one of the great eras of British pop, the same as they do with the Sixties. I think we are living through an enormous maelstrom of great new music."

This was best reflected by the so-called Britstock in Leeds for the Heineken Music Festival in July 1995. Whereas the previous year the line-up would have been dominated by introspective American guitar bands, now the entire bill consisted of acts like Pulp, Powder, Menswear, The Bluetones and Marion.

Certain older bands became fashionable influences again. The majority of the great British bands drew on the unique character of British life for their best songs. Just as The Sex Pistols laughed at the tabloids, The Jam detailed small town precincts and The Smiths mythologised the normality of life, now Blur and the new generation were hailing the good and bad in their home country. Many of the Britpop groups had grown up in Britain without the first hand clutter of punk, so its influence was barely involved, although some bands drew on its swagger for their live shows. More substantially, many of the Sixties groups cited as references for *Modern Life* and *Parklife* now enjoyed a renewed popularity. The Beatles couldn't have picked a better time to release their Anthology series, but of all the elder statesmen of British pop, it was Ray Davies to whom the Britpop bands owed the biggest vote of thanks, a fact that Damon would acknowledge in due course.

Vocally if not lyrically, Damon's so-called Mockney accent mirrored the Cockney Rebel Steve Harley and who else but Jarvis Cocker could sing about "wood chip" in a Sheffield accent? Cynics successfully argued that many of the Britpop contingent sounded too much like their influences,

Opposite Page: "The boy Damon
done good" Phil Daniels muses over
Blur's park life

a kind of 'spot the reference', slicing up history and
re-selling the same package. Defenders pointed to acts who
were re-inventing the past with their own dash of originality,
taking a pastiche and working it with enough intelligence
to create something fresh and new.

So 1994 was the year of Britpop's arrival, with Blur's
*Parklife* as the album of the year. But there was enormous
diversity in the scene. The peculiar English musical reference
points of Blur and Supergrass were hardly acceptable
influences for Radiohead. Pulp and Blur talked of a
behind-the-net curtains Britain, but Johnny-Come-Lately
Oasis didn't, neither did Marion. Elastica sounded as
much like Menswear as Nirvana did.

Also, the vital thing to remember is that none of
these bands really considered themselves to be part of a
movement. Some groups enjoyed success on the coat-tails
of the bigger bands, but that is the case with any musical
movement. Suede distanced themselves from Britpop hastily,
as did Marion. Oasis refused to appear on the BBC2
documentary entitled *Britpop Now* although Damon
presented it and Pulp, Elastica and Menswear appeared.
Britpop remains a convenient label for a rich new seam
of British talent.

Britpop *is* a media fiction and crucially an industry
compatible one, as Gilbert explains: "At the same time that
Britpop has parallels with punk in terms of removing the
old guard, whilst punk was a revolutionary force, Britpop is
a very reactionary force. It fits into the industry, it is very
tied up with commercialism and selling records. Britpop
doesn't threaten anyone, it benefits everyone, and it doesn't
pose any threat to society – it's not drug oriented, it's
not socially subversive, it is a phenomenon because it isn't
a threat."

Only one thing is certain. By the end of 1996 Britpop
will be past its sell-by date. Musical movements and trends
enjoy cyclical success and inevitably Britpop will be
dethroned by something new. Until then, it has given a much
needed boost to British pop for which fans, bands and
everyone else should be grateful.

• • •

As publicly elected leaders of the pack, Blur became
unavoidably involved with certain sociological aspects of
Britpop. There was the emergence of the so-called New Lad,
born to rebel against the tide of political correctness.
Perhaps the most visible aspect of this trend was the launch
of the hugely successful magazine *Loaded*, whose motto was
"For men who should know better" and whose pages were
filled with football, beer, bimbos and bands. *Fantasy Football*
made a similarly amazing breakthrough, despite John Major
railing against the "yob culture". Blur were not unaffected
by all this – Damon spoke out against PC and many of their
interviews in 1994 were about football and beer drinking.
Alex was involved in a drunken brawl at a Menswear

gig after he shouted "I shagged your sister" to the drummer
from the band Panic. Damon even contributed an article to
a programme for his beloved Chelsea FC . Neither was he
averse to strictly un-PC language: "As far as bisexuality goes,
I've had a little taste of that fruit, or I've been tasted, you
might say. But when you get down to it, you can't beat a good
pair of tits."

This laddishness was also apparent during various
appearances at celebrity football matches and visits to
The Good Mixer in Camden Town, official home to many of
the drinking bands (including the ultimate lads band, Oasis).
Damon told *Select*: "It's necessary to have a comic fill to the
whole politically correct revolution. That's what the New Lad
is… it's a way of expressing the more visceral side of being
a human being in this age." Graham was less convinced,
and found it embarrassing when "Parklife" became a yob
chant that now represented much of this new attitude.

Unfortunately, the more toxic side of being a New Lad
caused Damon much ill health, a problem severe enough for
him to require professional medical help. Damon claimed
never to have felt depressed before, even during the band's
worst times, but here he was, standing astride British pop's
throne and he was waking up unhappy. Clearly, Blur's
enormous work load around *Parklife* didn't help but the
heavy drinking and occasional cocaine use brought on
insomnia. With the public eye suddenly focused on Blur,
it was a real culture shock: "I had to grow up in public
in 1994, because I was still a teenager at the age of 26,"
said Damon.

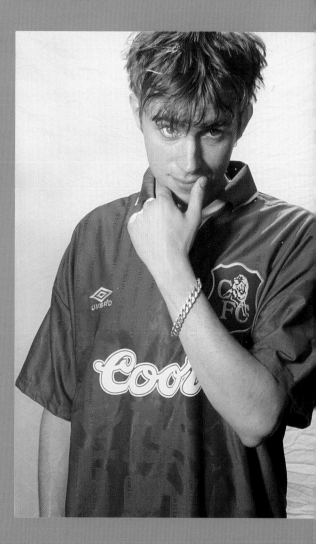

"A sane pop person"

He was now regularly crying, unsatisfied, depressed and angry, and the occasional incidence of depression in his family history unnerved him even more. He became something of a hypochondriac, worrying about shoulder pains and even heart disease. By the time he was performing 'To The End' on *Top of the Pops* he couldn't cope and was desperately unhappy. He attended a Harley Street doctor who told him that his cocaine use had affected his nervous system and combined with the heavy drinking had caused various health problems. He was given anti-depressant tablets and sent away, the doctor's warning that it could be up to a year before he was fully recovered ringing in his ears.

Damon stopped taking drugs after two days and decided to change his lifestyle. Cocaine and coffee were outlawed and the drinking was cut back, and he even went to a gym occasionally. Of the cocaine Damon told *The Face*: "I don't think that was the problem, but I stopped and I'd be very reluctant to do it again. Although I loved it, it was idiotic.

"When Kurt Cobain killed himself I thought I was having a nervous breakdown, which I wasn't at all. I felt very disturbed by his death and it did haunt me for a while. But in 1994 I realised that I can do this, and that you can be fairly-level headed about it and not go mad."

His six months of neurosis dealt with in typically pragmatic style, Damon seemed capable of hanging on to his old self with engaging ease. He had undergone the transition from a sane person to what he called "a sane pop person" with fewer scars than most.

● ● ●

So in the end, Blur made it to the close of their most successful year to date with relatively few problems. Despite a last minute flurry from Oasis with their début album *Definitely Maybe*, Blur's fourth album was far more historically significant. It had resurrected British music and renewed interest in young and old native bands alike.

"Drinking was cut back..."

Handsomely supported by Britpop's cast, Blur had successfully led a British retaliation against the American invaders.

There was a litany of victories along the way. *Parklife* made a clean sweep of just about all the major end of year music polls. They took the prestigious Q Album of the Year Award while *Smash Hits* Awards by the bag full confirmed the lasting cross-over had been made into the massive teen market. Even when they lost the Mercury Award, their record sales shot up by 125% in the next two weeks. *Parklife* hit platinum sales within its first week of release and did not fall out of the Top 20 from then until the New Year. Part of the longevity of this success was Blur's astute single releases, with each new record drawing different people into the experience. 'Girls & Boys' was adult pop, 'To The End' won over many of the 30-something CD public which had made Mick Hucknall a multi-millionaire, 'Parklife' was a comical appeal to the younger generation and 'To The End' covered all the bases.

The band's status as celebrities rocketed. They attended film premières and Alex snogged supermodels (he denies anything more serious with Helena Christiensen). Damon scooped virtually all the 'Sexiest Man of the Year' awards, despite Justine saying "he has one of the lowest sex drives of any man I have ever met. He's not that into sex." They were asked to record a theme tune for the 1996 European Championships by the FA, along with Oasis. *Spitting Image* did a Blur take-off of the troubled Prince Charles called "Charles Life" and Martin Amis asked for a copy of their album after having read that it was a sonic version of his acclaimed novel *London Fields*.

Biffo, a close friend of the band, has seen their success arrive and noted how they have maintained their normality: "Damon sees Blur as his brainchild and so he is always willing to talk about it, but he does not like the intrusion into his private life. As the lead singer whose girlfriend is also famous, this has caused some trouble with idle gossip. Graham is still a very shy man, and he hates the attention that his fame has brought. When we go out we find places we know he will not be recognised, and he really dislikes any public exposure of his private life. Alex is still Alex, the same as he was when they first started. Being so intellectual, he finds that people are wary of that and he will play up to it, teasing them. Dave is quieter now, he is not into the partying so much, he loves his flying and is still very much into computers. It amazes me how they have been able to keep that four brothers mentality going, and don't seem to have picked up any of the trappings of big pop stars."

Even Blur's problems during this fantastic period were turned to their advantage with panache. Some saw the *Parklife* album artwork as glamorising the sport of greyhound racing. Betting slips were now constantly thrown on stage at Blur gigs, and one Japanese version of *Parklife* barked when you opened the case while the dog's eyes on the cover lit up when pressed. Some were not impressed – one letter to a weekly paper raged: "Don't buy anything by Blur – they sanction the killing of defenceless animals." Blur were a little taken aback by the extent of the criticism, and subsequently paid for a retired greyhound to be put in kennels for a year. More publicly, they paid for a joint poster campaign with The Canine Defence League which showed a dog with the legend "Not just for Christmas" alongside the band's album cover. It was a clever manoeuvre which negated much of the anger.

The year long media campaign bordered on over-exposure. Hundreds of articles saw Damon's headline-grabbing skills blossom as the country's new mercurial pop genius. They appealed to teen magazines as easily as they did to *GQ* and *Modern Review* (in which Damon wrote a piece about yob culture, comically the same week that Alex was being featured in *The Daily Star* as a star drunk), and they appeared on *Later With Jools Holland* as comfortably as they did on European tea time television. One particular incident saw them play *Top Of The Pops*, then head off to Stringfellows only to be refused admittance because they were carrying Tesco bags. Peter Stringfellow had previously branded them drunken louts and said they weren't welcome in his club: "I found them to be the most obnoxious little shits I have had in my club for a long while."

The biggest achievements of all were at The Brit Awards ceremony at Alexandra Palace, the scene of Blur's greatest triumph. Blur scooped a record- breaking four awards for Best Album, Video, Single and Best Band. For the last acceptance speech, Alex said that Oasis should have received the award with them jointly. With Damon's previous *Top Of The Pops* recommendation ("This is Oasis and they are wonderful"), maybe this was the start of a long and happy friendship?

Just after this awards scoop Blur were invited on to *Top Of The Pops* where Damon played keyboards for Elastica before running over to the opposite stage for Blur's rendition of 'Jubilee'. For this performance, Dave had painted his first name on his cheek as a 'tribute' to The Artist Formerly Known As Prince, who in recent weeks had made several public appearances with 'Slave' scrawled on his face, apparently in protest against his Warner Brothers record contract. Said Dave: "I was considering writing 'wanka' on my face but it wouldn't fit. I have changed my name to The Drummer Formerly Known As Dave. I did it because Karen at the record company told me to. Me and Prince have got a lot in common – EMI won't release my solo album either."

*Parklife* had crystallised everything that Blur were about, and on a commercial scale EMI were astonished at its success and the strength of Blur's comeback from the lows of 1992. The band were also understandably delighted with the year's work – no-one had realised just how massively their album was going to succeed. Damon said to *NME:* "I don't think there's another band that have qualified what they are about in the world as much as we have. We have come to a point where we've met our market full on. I know it will change, but right now, it's all ours. When we started I really wanted to be part of something, but we are out on our own now. Untouchable."

Alex similarly mixed pride with pragmatism in *NME* when he said: "We've had a good year. It's time for the bubble to burst, or maybe for us to get bigger. 1994 has been very busy, very disturbed, very paranoid, very dangerous – but the best year of my whole life."

Brit Awards 1995,
before, during and after

# 10

## Everything's Going Jackanory

Blurmania continued into 1995 whilst the band were already writing and demo-ing new material for the next album. Damon appeared on *The White Room* to sing 'Waterloo Sunset' with Ray Davies, after The Kinks frontman had been on a European TV show with them and liked their material. Damon didn't care that the impromptu 'Parklife' they also sang was rather painful, and later told *NME*: "This is one of the most exciting things I've done. He is as much an influence as anyone else for me. He's fundamentally a part of what I do. What he did is just in my blood, it's a part of my upbringing." Of Davies' most famous song Damon said: "Without a shadow of a doubt, it is the most perfect song I could ever wish to write."

"You're enjoying it now, but wait 'til we sing 'Parklife!'"

Damon's childhood interest in 2-Tone led to his working with Terry Hall at the start of the year, along with the enigmatic Tricky, on some material for the latter's new project Durban Poison. The cosmopolitan Tricky had also been a rude boy in his youth, so there was much common ground. Damon's contribution, 'I'll Pass Right Through You', was eventually removed from the record at his own request. Damon also appeared on an Amnesty International video called "Use Your Freedom" alongside Gary Lineker and Andy Peters which coincided with the 34th anniversary of the organisation.

Blur won several *NME* Brat awards and shared the limelight uncomfortably with Oasis, and then played a short but blistering three song set at The Forum for the corresponding live show. Damon also made a special guest appearance with The Pretenders at an acoustic show in London, joining Chrissie Hynde on piano for a version of Ray Davies' 'I Go To Sleep', and even edited the *NME* for a week. Absolute fame and fortune were finally guaranteed with a cartoon series on Blur in the *News Of The World*

Sunday magazine, whose readership was over 11 million. Although a little factually incorrect, the captions were hilarious: "Four lads from Essex, unheard of a year ago, have blown pop apart to become Britain's hottest band. Blur have catapulted to instant stardom." So 1995 had begun as 1994 ended – how would it progress?

● ● ●

The new campaign started well with Britpop's finest hour, Blur's 27,000 seat show at Mile End stadium in London's East End on Saturday June 17. First, there was an amazingly shambolic warm-up date at Camden's Dublin Castle, arguably the smallest London venue on the circuit. Understandably, due to the size of the gig, and the fact it was Blur's first UK show since selling out 7,000 tickets at the Ally Pally, the 200 or so tickets were in ridiculous demand and secrecy was paramount. Despite having been regular giggers at the trendy Camden Falcon, Blur had never actually played the nearby Dublin Castle, and because of its size and bad PA the show had to revolve around the more punky numbers, although two new songs were also aired, 'Globe Alone' and 'Stereotypes'. Regardless of the technical difficulties, it was an extraordinary event, one of Britain's biggest bands playing one of the country's smallest venues.

It was all a far cry from the massive shows they were now used to playing, and for that reason the band loved it. Several celebrities were in attendance, including Elastica, Pulp and Menswear (who claimed listening to Blur had made them form a band in the first place – they later recorded a spoof Western track called '26 Years' especially for Graham's birthday).

The day of the Mile End gig finally arrived and so did the summer rain. It was a grey, windy and overcast East End that greeted the thousands of Blur fans, but this did nothing to dampen spirits. Outside the venue, fears were expressed about large gatherings of skinheads and Hell's Angels, but nothing unsavoury transpired. Inside the stadium, the cast of pop celebrities was endless, and even Prince Edward was rumoured to be in attendance. The Shanakies opened the show and made life difficult for a drab Cardiacs, whose set paled in comparison to the hard guitar driven music of the openers. After that, Dodgy confirmed their place among the country's finest bands, then the newly fashionable Sparks played their quirky electro pop to a mixed response. Neither they nor the Cardiacs seemed entirely appropriate for the day. There were no such reservations when The Boo Radleys took to the stage – in the past they had played their fair share of awful live shows, but now the songs that gave them a No. 1 album with *Wake Up Boo* were greeted wildly, and whetted the crowd's appetite for the show to come.

Red flares signalled the start of the second half of the show, but the double-decker bus which Blur were rumoured to be driving on stage never appeared. Instead Damon entered in a false head, fake pot-belly and business suit for the opening 'Tracy Jacks', set against the backdrop of giant hamburgers, neon lights and video screens. Only three new songs were aired, the two from the Dublin Castle show and a third one called 'Country House', but despite the scarcity of new material, no-one minded. This was Blur's moment, the peak of their career to date, and nothing could take that away from them. Phil Daniels emerged from a box marked 'Daniels' to perform yet another 'last ever' rendition of 'Parklife' and the encores of 'Daisy Bell' and 'This Is A Low' closed the night. It would be difficult for Blur to top this.

As if to confirm their ability to perform on this level, Blur supported R.E.M. at the massive Milton Keynes Bowl in late July. Blur flew in by helicopter, and despite initial reservations about such shows, they performed well and seemed comfortable with the huge surroundings. Doubts that their quirky English soundscapes would translate to a stage that often demanded bland sloganeering proved groundless, although the jingo-istic chants of "Enger-land" that worryingly followed Blur everywhere were again present. This was very much R.E.M.'s gig, hardly America's finest, being challenged by Britain's champions (as some suggested Damon wanted it to be), but it nevertheless confirmed the arena-filling potential seen at Mile End.

One criticism of Blur at this time was that by focusing and mimicking their lifestyles they were manipulating the working class for their own gain. The subject of class has plagued Blur almost since their inception, and they've been derided as middle class softies toying with working class imagery. The band's further education (even though they attended comprehensive not private schools) and particularly Damon's fascination with literature is seen as contrary to working class sensibility.

Damon has claimed never to have read a rock biography and instead hailed many literary greats. He thanked Herman Hesse, Lobsang Rampas and D H Lawrence on the sleeve notes for *Leisure*. He paraphrased Beckett in 'Repetition'. Even their T-shirts, often the reserve of 'fuck you' statements, were emblazoned with book covers of classics like 'The Thin Man'. Despite failing his A-levels, Damon was quickly picked up as a pop intellectual and his own comments reinforced this view: "Herman Hesse was the first writer who actually had any effect on me. He was always trying to define a spirituality but at the same time he stayed clear of any sex or dogma. He was one of the first urban pagans." For *Modern Life Is Rubbish* Damon cited Douglas Coupland's *Generation X* as his key inspiration, and he went on to revere Martin Amis' *London Fields* novel for *Parklife*.

Despite this intellectualism, they played gigs in the East End, drew on music hall (which was always heavily associated with the East End) and Damon openly exaggerated his accent for dramatic affect. For many,

"Despite his chirpy demeanour, fame had taken its toll on Damon's good looks"

Triumphant at Mile End, June 1995

this was like Mick Jagger, a middle class boy who convinced the world he was an East End yob, when all he was really doing was feigning a working class persona. To some Blur will never be real lads, real working class, nor real East Enders. Unless Damon cops a GBH conviction, forms a new band called The Bootleg Kinks and takes up a job selling jellied eels in Bethnal Green market, maybe he will never be accepted for real.

Damon has readily admitted he is fascinated by working class lives, but claims that his work is much wider in scope than that – he feels that the broader focus of *Parklife* was often missed: "Not all the characters are bloody working class, the majority of that record concerns itself with the worst things I hate about middle class people. The only real references to working class culture are the cover of the album, the greyhounds, but too much has been made of that image."

At the Mile End show he said: "I'd better make sure I haven't got a cockney accent 'cos I'm not allowed." He now dismisses the issue as tedious: "There was a time when any pop star who even admitted to enjoying books was dismissed as a middle class twat. They've virtually given up calling me that because I have actually admitted 'Yes, I am a middle class twat!'"

•  •  •

Blur had been working on their new album since late 1994, and by the New Year they had 30 songs in demo form. This created problems in itself, as they had to constantly switch from writing new work to promoting the still-active *Parklife*. In keeping with their ceaseless work ethic, the third album in three years was completed ahead of schedule, recording at a consistent rate of three songs per week. Alex explains: "There's no mystery why we've got better, we just work hard. Very few bands work as hard as we do, and if you work very hard you will get better. I don't think it's about being clever. Academic cleverness doesn't really come into pop music."

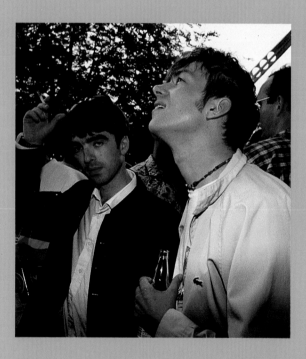

Middle class wanker
with working class hero?

Stephen Street agreed, as he told *Mojo*: "They are incredibly prolific. All the great acts have gone through a period of intense creativity, like Bowie in the early RCA years and The Smiths who produced a load of great singles as well as albums." One major benefit of this prolific nature is that Blur's B-sides have always offered interesting diversions from the lead track – 'Peach' (from the 'For Tomorrow' single) is just one of many examples of a flip side track that was easily strong enough to be released as a single in its own right.

Deciding which tracks finally made it onto the fourth album was difficult – deciding the first single was a lot easier.

The response to 'Country House' at Mile End had been overwhelming, so it immediately usurped 'Stereotypes' as the taster for the new record. It was a jaunty pop song with a dark lyrical sub-text that made it a stand-out, addictive Blur single. The scene was set in a country mansion Damon had visited in Suffolk as a child, and concerned an escapee from the rat race who survives on Prozac and panic attacks – twelve months ago this could easily have been Damon. Its obvious mass appeal also made it a perfect contender to follow up *Parklife*.

Unfortunately, the considerable musical merits of the new single were lost amid the furore that erupted when Oasis' single 'Roll With It' was released simultaneously on August 14, creating what was dubbed 'The Battle of Britain'. With a seemingly endless supply of classic pop singles and a smash début album, Oasis had won popular approval at a startling rate. Add to that their boozy, drugged excess and the Gallagher Brothers volatile relationship and Britain was captivated. Glastonbury headline slots and three No. 1 singles were accomplished with swaggering Mancunian arrogance. When Oasis released their first single 'Supersonic', Blur were preparing to release *Parklife* – now the Mancunian band were a very serious threat to Blur's British music supremacy.

Their relationship with Blur had started off well, with Damon championing their cause several times, but things soon started to turn sour. In The Good Mixer one night, Liam spotted Graham and harangued him so much he was thrown out – the ceaseless berating continued in The Underworld Club. At an autumn 1994 radio interview in San Francisco, both bands were booked by a conniving radio station at the same time, and the only greetings exchanged were "Wanker" and "Geezer". Liam had initially said "Blur are a top band", but at the Brat Awards photo sessions he refused to be snapped alongside Damon. Although Noel gladly took part, Liam was later incensed when Graham sneaked a kiss on his cheek, and from that moment on the two parties were at each other's throats. Noel retracted his earlier praise of Blur, saying he had been out of his head on drugs at the time. So when it was announced that both bands were to release their new singles from new albums on the same day, the battle lines were drawn.

The battle, like Britpop itself, was fuelled by the media. The bands have to take a large portion of the blame, because they didn't *have* to take part, they could have changed release dates. Opposing sides claim the others caused the fight, but the truth is that Damon called the clash after Liam was abusive to him at a celebration party for Oasis' No. 1 single 'Some Might Say'. So the rough Northerners with a No. 1 single lined up against the art school Londoners with a No. 1 album, a cupboard full of awards, but no No. 1 single. Some said it was the biggest battle since the days of The Beatles and The Rolling Stones, but these two legends had in fact staggered their releases for mutual benefit – the many singles both bands released did not clash once. The Clash and The Sex Pistols, and The Stone Roses and The Happy Mondays were always plagued by rumours of rivalry, but nothing from those periods eclipsed this.

One, two, three and turn...

Gallagher brothers

in a rare "mouth shut" moment

Blur seemed more equipped for battle than Oasis. They had fake estate agents' boards pronouncing 'For Sale: Country House. Enquire Within' erected outside London record shops. When Damon appeared on Chris Evans' Radio 1 morning show, he sang Status Quo's 'Rockin' All Over The World' over the lead line of Oasis' track, and christened them Oasis Quo. Blur's formatting was more astute, with live versions of Mile End tracks being available on alternative CD's, causing many people to buy two singles, whereas Oasis could only offer £1 off. Damon was also anxious to remind the public who had been around the longest, as he told *Melody Maker*: "As far as I can see, Oasis have everything to gain and nothing to lose. Everything for them is just a bonus now, they're a household name now and I don't think they were before."

Blur's video was far more entertaining than Oasis' rather dry black and white performance footage. Damien Hirst, the acclaimed Turner Prize-winning artist (he of the sheep in formaldehyde fame) directed what was a bizarre Benny Hill on acid style promo, complete with busty page three girls, surreal board game and general cavorting and titillation. Hirst had attended Goldsmiths' with Alex and Graham and had even considered managing Blur after seeing them perform at a College exhibition where he was showing his latest piece of art, a cupboard full of medicine. He had not really noticed their success until bumping into them at the celebrity haunt The Groucho Club one night and realising he went to school with them. The sexual overtones and tabloid nature of this video perfectly fitted the nature of the week's mayhem and received considerably more airplay than Oasis' offering.

Oasis chose to play the 'We're so hard we'll be No. 1' card. They had opened the stakes by premièring their single at Glastonbury to 100,000 people, but after that they were less direct. Less flashy videos, less subtle media manipulation

and decidedly less subtle soundbites – Noel said to one paper: "Blur are a bunch of middle class wankers trying to play hardball with a bunch of working class heroes." They encouraged people to buy the single, saying it wouldn't be on the album, which of course it was. For the whole week they were touring Japan as well, which put them at a distinct disadvantage. Still, they had a massive database of 130,000 fans and had already achieved the No. 1 spot, unlike Blur.

Both bands were shocked by the media hysteria that took hold the week of release. Despite continued atrocities in Bosnia, VJ Day and Mike Tyson's release from prison, all the tabloids were involved with *The Daily Sport* producing the best headline of "Blur Job". All the major television stations joined in, with even the *Six O'Clock News* running a feature. Magazines as far away as Brazil were phoning up to get the latest, and bookies reported brisk business on the outcome.

It rapidly became a wider issue than just the music. According to some, this was north *vs* south, middle class *vs* working class, rock *vs* pop, intelligence *vs* brawn. It was also EMI *vs* Sony, Food *vs* Creation, even one press agent against another. Tabloids battled for scoops with 0891 phone-ins, and the resulting haste produced much misinformation, including one story about mods against rockers.

All week it was neck and neck, with contrasting reports from media sources and record shops claiming first one band then the other were in front. Blur went into retreat. Damon was on holiday with his parents in Mauritius. Dave had been okay at first but as the week progressed he couldn't sleep, so he flew to France with his wife. Graham went AWOL for the week – he hated the whole ludicrous affair, and even thought about buying 300 copies of each single to sabotage the contest. He later told *NME*: "I went into a state of shock and I don't think I got out of it. It's a circle of freaks and I don't want to be involved in it." Only Alex seemed more than happy to stay at home and watch the spectacle develop. Despite withdrawing from the frenzy, Blur were by now desperate to win. Damon told *The Face*: "If I come back on Sunday and we're not No. 1 someone is going to suffer some sort of grievous bodily harm. We haven't had a No. 1 and they wouldn't have if we hadn't got the ball rolling in the first place. We exhumed the corpse of pop music."

Damon needn't have worried – when the charts were announced on Sunday evening, 'Country House' hit No. 1, with Oasis straight in at No. 2. Record sales had hit their highest peak for ten years, and of the 1.8 million singles sold, nearly 500,000 were these two. Blur outsold Oasis by 22%, 270,000 to 220,000. The Battle Of Britain domination had taken over so much that Britain's biggest selling pop band Take That were easily dethroned, and Madonna's new single went virtually unnoticed. Blur's triumph was reinforced by hitting No. 1 in Ireland, Belgium and Portugal.

Obviously Blur were delighted. Dave misleadingly said: "I never had the slightest doubt that we were gonna get to No. 1" and Damon said: "These are great times, anything's possible. Do Blur deserve it? Of course we do." The truth is there was great relief in the Blur camp. *Parklife* had been o upstage its memory. It needed this media overkill and fictitious battle to supersede the previous album and prepare for the next album. Graham was relieved but still unhappy, he hated the tackiness of the video and left the band's own celebration party early (he didn't even attend the EMI party for the band). Blur were graceful in victory, with Alex wearing an Oasis T-shirt for their triumphant *Top Of The Pops* appearance, of which he told *NME*: "It was a magnanimous gesture. I think that they are a great band and that this is the defining moment of Britpop. It's not Blur *versus* Oasis, it's Blur and Oasis *versus* the world."

The media scam that the battle had become was highlighted by the lack of animosity between rival fans and the fact that many people bought both singles. Whether it was a scam or not is irrelevant – everyone won, the bands, the press, the record shops, the record companies, it was a very positive event, however superficial. And in a year dominated by the pop anti-Christs of Robson & Jerome, few would argue.

Noel Gallagher was devastated he hadn't achieved his long time ambition of beating his hero Paul Weller's tally of four No. 1 singles. The Oasis camp claimed they had experienced bar code problems, leaving thousands of sales unregistered – this smelt of sour grapes, but Oasis would not be down for long. With Blur now reigning apparently unchallenged at the top of the charts, many observers felt they could now go on to even greater success by winning the album war, while Oasis' more one dimensional guitar pop would suffer badly from having lost. They could not have been more wrong.

● ● ●

"The best record you can make is recorded on Monday, cut on Tuesday, pressed on Wednesday, packaged on Thursday, distributed on Friday and in the shops on Saturday." So said John Lennon, and this ultimate punk ethic was the inspiration for the War Child charity album *Help,* released in early September. Blur joined Paul McCartney, Oasis, Paul Weller, Radiohead, Suede and others to raise funds for medical supplies, food and shelter for children affected by the Bosnian conflict. Blur's contribution was recorded during tour dates in Milan, and was originally titled 'I Hope You Find Your Suburbs' but later changed to 'Eine Kleine Lift Muzak'. The album sold massively but because of the rules governing compilation records, it was refused a position in the main album chart.

At this point, as Blur were busy preparing for the release of the new album, there was a dramatic acceleration in the war of words with Oasis. Liam Gallagher, not the subtlest of suitors, claimed that Justine Frischmann, Damon's girl, actually fancied a bit of rough with him, that he could no longer suppress his lustful feelings towards her and that it was his intention to seduce her. The music press saw the humour in the situation and played it up, while an embarrassed Justine coolly ignored Liam when he insulted her – by yelling "get yer tits out" – at an awards ceremony.

Unfortunately, the whole rivalry reached a pitiful nadir

when Noel told *The Observer* magazine that he hoped "Alex and Damon caught Aids and died". Outrage and anger ensued, and Andy Ross of Food Records said: "This is supposed to be the clever one talking." Eventually Noel was forced to write an apology, in which he said: "Although not being a fan of their music, I wish both Damon and Alex a long and healthy life." Some said that on top of the singles defeat, this comment would maybe kill Oasis, in the same way The Happy Mondays homophobic comments in their heyday had hastened their own demise.

For Damon the situation was now out of hand, as he told *Melody Maker*: "When the whole thing started with them, it was quite fun. Prior to the whole thing we got on quite well, there was the sense that things were going great for both bands. Now the whole war of words has just left me sad, it just got so ugly." The media would not let go however, and continued to bait both bands. The chart war will probably plague both acts for ever, but the personal venom between them has already dissipated. Ric Blaxill of *Top Of The Pops* gave a telling insight into the Oasis/Blur war when they both appeared on his show in early 1996: "One of the finest recent performances on the show was Blur's 'Stereotypes', just before Oasis went on stage for their two numbers. For the whole song Liam was dancing along in the crowd, he was really enjoying himself. Afterwards in the bar he and Damon were chatting away merrily, they certainly weren't going at each other's throats. Both bands seemed to get on very well."

"Nice hat, geezer"
"Cheers, wanker"

# 11

## Best Days

How do you follow the biggest album of the decade? The pressure has stifled some bands – The Stone Roses spring to mind – but Blur were hard at work in the studio while *Parklife* was still riding high in the charts. Stephen Street was again at the controls. "In him you have The Smiths and Blur and as far as I am concerned that's the Eighties and Nineties taken care of," said Damon. Street wasn't surprised that Blur were back at work again. "They give you so much good material in the first place, you'd have to be a complete moron to bugger up the production on a Blur album," he told *Melody Maker*.

Blur's fourth album, *The Great Escape*, completed a trilogy of records on the same theme. Released on September 11, 1995, it was a highly detailed, multi-faceted record which took a more cosmopolitan angle on the suburban dystopia of the previous two records. Musically, the record was Graham's masterpiece, and Street loudly declared him to be on a par with Johnny Marr. As well as five guitars, Graham also played baritone and soprano sax and banjo, and also contributed many backing vocals. He swayed from the stabbing riffs that opened 'Stereotypes' to the punk pop of 'Charmless Man' or the aggressive 'Globe Alone', and the string style backing for the elegant 'The Universal'. Even on 'Country House', superficially a straightforward pop song, Graham's dextrous textures gave the track great depth and colour. Perhaps most fascinating was his minimalist style: what he missed out was as important as what he put in. Alex's bass was impressive too – his odd lazy rhythms informed 'Fade Away', 'Country House', 'It Could Be You' and 'The Universal', which had been around at the time of *Parklife* in an undeveloped reggae/calypso format, but reappeared here as a lush sad ode. Dave proved to be a living metronome again, with faster rolls, more dynamics and more variation than on previous Blur records. This was vital since the sonic variety of the record demanded a rigid and absolutely perfect rhythm section.

*The Great Escape* was chock full of odd sounds, taking it way beyond the range of traditional pop. 'Ernold Same' featured MP Ken Livingstone droning on about the rat race, with noises from the Goldhawk Road and a local swimming bath doubling up as a train station. Odd whirling organs flew all across the record, especially on 'Stereotypes' and 'Mr Robinson's Quango'. 'Fade Away' was eerie and melancholic with sad trombones describing the weariness of a dying marriage. 'He Thought Of Cars', although rather cluttered, is a sad and desperate tale filled with painful guitars and quirky organs. 'Top Man' has comically deep backing vocals mixed with happy whistling, while 'Best Days' has contrasting android backing vocals. On 'Yuko and Hiro' the Casio-tones and muzak instruments take over completely on a lament full of eerie space-age noise. Generally, this was a more programmed album than any previous work by Blur, and the musical textures far surpassed even the broad palette of *Parklife*.

The influences were still there. The Specials were clearly important to 'Fade Away' and Damon readily admitted that 'Top Man' was a direct result of his recent writing work with Terry Hall. Madness could be heard in the piano, and The Style Council's 'Life At A Top People's Health Farm' was mirrored by 'Country House'. The sonic experiments recalled at various moments Sparks, Wire, Brian Eno and Kraftwerk. Generally, this was a far less derivative record than its predecessor, with the Blur sound established in its own right, without the need to refer elsewhere. Steve Harley said as much when he met Blur backstage and later reported his meeting on the Internet: "This is proof if needed that regardless of all the myriad merciless comparisons with others, some of whose careers peaked before three of the band were born, Blur have found their own place in modern pop."

The 'Stereotypes' and 'Country House' tracks were misleading in that they were typical Blur-by-numbers. 'Country House' was thankfully the only concession to the knees up mode that had featured so heavily on *Parklife*. Elsewhere they were producing music that had hardly been hinted at before, with close attention to detail on tune upon tune. Somehow, they managed to keep the complex mass of ideas simple and direct, and much of the credit lies with Graham's arrangements.

Lyrically, many tracks pursued Damon's characteristic third person voyeurism. Most of the lyrics were written on the roof top balcony of the house in west London he shared with Justine, and with the pressure of *Parklife*, he found this task harder than any other on the album project. The new characters were similarly disenchanted types, but more sexually active and deviant than on *Parklife*. 'Mr Robinson's Quango' was a tragi-comedy about a council worker who dressed in stockings and suspenders under his suit, inspired by a graffiti confession Damon once read on a train station toilet door. 'Stereotypes' hailed the pleasures of wife-swapping and 'Entertain Me' (originally titled 'Bored Wives') details a bored middle aged man looking for relief by flagellation. 'Yuko and Hiro' tells of an over-worked Japanese employee struggling to control his life and dreaming about the girlfriend he never sees, a thinly veiled comment on his relationship with Justine (they saw each other for only three weeks in 1995; they even split up temporarily over the Christmas period).

Some said 'Country House' was about Dave Balfe, the ex-Food Records partner who had since sold Food to EMI. Elsewhere there was talk of pointless marriages, friendless spongers, Prozac-addicted executives, the futility of the Lottery, boy racers, and even a character called Dan Abnormal. This was an anagram of Damon Albarn which Justine had thought up to mock her boyfriend, and he used it in a self-deprecating wander around the dull shopping arcades of life. Damon was still singing in his Thames Estuary vowels, but 'The Universal' showed that he was becoming an accomplished ballad singer.

It was a complex, sumptuously layered, and sonically complicated album, frequently eclectic, quirky, odd, queer, harsh and strange. Damon told *Mojo*: "We've always seen ourselves as putting on white coats and going into the lab" when asked about his attitude to recording the album, and it showed. He also spoke of their motivation to work hard when he told *NME*: "The pressures were strange. I've never had that thing about fame and making money. I just wanted to make something that I thought was good because I knew the attention this album would get."

*The Great Escape* is less immediate than *Parklife*. Indeed, many found it too hard listening, too labyrinthine, too complicated. Where *Parklife* had opted for easier targets, the cheap laughs of the sing-alongs, pub stomps, pure pop and softer instrumentation, *The Great Escape* was far more ambitious. It repeatedly sacrificed the obvious for the unusual. It was not crammed with hit singles, but that should never be the sole criteria for a classic album. In the context of following up *Parklife*, Blur should defy any of their peers to better *The Great Escape*. Indeed, it is far and away their most accomplished piece of work.

Stephen Street told *Music Week*: "It is a step on from *Parklife,* but it won't alienate anybody who got into Blur with it. It's a bit darker but I think that's the only way for us to go." Johnny Cigarettes in *NME* was more direct: "We can only demand a masterpiece, and they've damn near delivered it." Now all that remained was to see if the public agreed.

● ● ●

Initial response was promising – the album smashed in at No. 1 in the charts in the UK, and also in Iceland and Hong Kong, while across Europe it achieved Top 5 spots in most territories. By the end of October, less than two months after release, it had already passed one million sales world-wide. Reviews in the UK were generally very strong and platinum status came during the third week of October. When Blur announced a seaside tour, followed by their biggest ever arena tour, all tickets were sold out in hours.

With typical Blur panache, they performed two promotional events in the two weeks after the album release that reinforced the void between the linear style of so many of their contemporaries and their own colourful approach. Firstly, on September 15, they played on top of the roof of

the HMV shop in Oxford Street in London. Accompanied by a four man brass section, Blur played for 20 minutes while huge crowds gathered below. The last time this had happened was Echo & The Bunnymen in the mid-Eighties. At one point Damon dangled the microphone down to the crowd to sing along, then he risked death by skipping along the edge of the roof while record company bosses went into apoplexy below. Five tracks from the new album were played, then the spectacle finished off with 'Parklife'.

**"Entertain Me, Dan Abnormal"**

Opposite: Damon getting shirty by
the seaside

"Fans etc"

The second canny promotional event was a live daytime Radio 1 show at Broadcasting House, prestigious treatment not even afforded to The Smiths or The Stone Roses. To a hall filled largely with journalists, Blur played a blistering set from the album, then once off air launched into a punk rock set that ruffled a few of the mainstream feathers in attendance. Both these events are typical of the style with which Blur promote themselves – the live radio, the unexpected secret shows, the forthcoming seaside dates, the 'Country House' For Sale boards, even their adverts (the map of the East End for their Mile End show) reflect a creative panache that adds to the legend with each new idea.

The second single from the album, 'The Universal' was released in November to coincide with the various album dates. It was considered to be a genuine contender for the Christmas No. 1, especially with the two new songs 'Ultranol' and 'In Me' included. The festive top spot eventually went to Michael Jackson's 'Earth Song', with Mike Flowers Pops cover of Oasis' 'Wonderwall' a close second, and 'The Universal' reaching No. 5. Blur's ballad was accompanied by a sinister video which went some way to banishing the growing embarrassment felt at the comedy 'Country House' promo, which was by now considered a mistake.

Blur's fascination with all things British continued during their small tour of eight run-down coastal venues that hadn't seen action on this level since the Fifties bingo boom.

The gigs included Pier 39 in Cleethorpes, Eastbourne Floral Hall and Great Yarmouth Ocean Rooms. The idea was to offer intimate, unusual shows for the fans while at the same time Blur could warm up for their forthcoming arena tour. Opening in Cleethorpes the tour made its way around the coastline, cramming creaking old venues to bulging point with great success. The poor sound systems didn't seem to affect the celebratory atmosphere at these shows.

The problem came when the band were nearing Bournemouth. Oasis had originally been booked to play the same night, and there was great excitement at the prospect of a battle. Unfortunately, some fans took this literally and there were soon rumours of marauding Oasis fans planning to ruck with Blur supporters, whose ranks were apparently going to be swelled by scores of Wolverhampton thugs down for the fight. The situation could have turned very nasty, and Oasis and Blur's offices swapped worried phone calls in search of a solution, their concern fuelled by the police's refusal to put extra officers on duty. Eventually Oasis, furious at Blur's intransigence, were forced to change their date. Blur were disappointed for more trivial reasons. They had planned to shine their logo Batman-like on the walls of Oasis' venue, and even hoped to have a huge inflatable 'No. 1' floating in the sky above.

During the winter schedule, Blur signed their official *Blurbook* photo collection at Books etc in Charing Cross Road on November 14. Over 2,000 kids queued for up to nine hours, but only about 750 books were signed as Blur had to rush across town for another appearance on *Later With Jools Holland*. The period was so busy that a proposed long form video entitled 'B Roads' had to be postponed from its original December 1995 release date until spring 1996, by which time it would include all of their world tour. The tour footage will be complemented by interviews with road protesters, a one-off Blur show for Eastbourne pensioners, 'kinky' housewives, and international storyteller Taffy Thomas.

By the time the seaside dates were complete, Blur's arena tour had swelled to 14 dates through huge ticket demand. Two additional Wembley Arena dates meant that by Christmas Blur would have played to over 180,000 on this leg of the tour alone. At one stage the media were suggesting that Blur should play Wembley Stadium, although the band made a statement distancing themselves from the spiral of bigger and bigger concerts, with Damon saying: "Wembley Stadium is for wankers! That's my last word."

Damon felt that Blur were ideal for the arena stages as he told *NME*: "We made the step up at Mile End, that was the best gig we've ever done. These shows will be like that except they're indoors so it won't rain. We feel quite comfortable in those venues, they seem quite intimate to us." The stage set itself was an amusement arcade right from one of the seaside venues they had just played, complete with flashing lights, a mirror ball and neon decorations. During 'The Universal', several giant Prozac tablets appeared above the band. To coincide with the resurgence of easy listening, Blur were supported by an unnamed MOR orchestra (whose members changed each night) who played cover versions of songs by Pulp, Oasis and Supergrass amongst others.

With the addition of a brass section and keyboard player, the renditions of mostly *Parklife* and *Great Escape* material were impressively accurate. Damon took to the bigger stage with consummate ease, using all his acting ability to present pure theatre to match the musical excellence. The best night was reserved for Wembley Arena's last show, when they were joined on stage by Phil Daniels for another 'last-ever' performance of '*Parklife*'. Both he and Damon dressed up in full pantomime regalia for that added Christmas feel.

The band were now living more healthy lives on tour and this showed in their performances. A vegetarian Damon was into jogging, and all except Alex performed Tae Kwon Do before each gig. Alex saved his energy for the bottle of champagne he sipped on stage at each show. Since 1992 an established band rule of 'no drinks 30 minutes before a show' had been in force.

Blur also seemed much more mature personally, as Damon told *Melody Maker:* "It's that sense of everything being normal and levelling out that's changed us. I used to spend so much time thinking the whole world revolved around me, that I was destined for great things, but not anymore." He publicly repudiated things he had said about Suede and said he felt they were under-rated and mistreated by the press. Even his normally arrogant statements were now injected with a dash of humour... "By 1999 we will be the most important band in the world... and also the moon. And maybe Mars." Despite this far more laid back approach, the new Blur weren't always on their best behaviour – one top London hotel banned them after riotous drunken behaviour left one guest fuming: "Nobody in the place knew who they were and they were just scruffy and noisy."

This arena tour confirmed that Blur were now mega-stars in the UK, capable of filling the nation's biggest sheds and playing a two hour set of classic songs. The teenage front rows graduated back to the 30 and 40 somethings at the back and the spread of reviews for each show confirmed an absolute cross-over between teen, alternative, music and mainstream media. Even John 'Spock' Redwood, one time Tory leader candidate and now full time loony, wrote about Blur in *The Guardian*, EastEnder tearaway Robbie wanted a 'Damon' haircut and Harry Enfield ridiculed them in his "Oi! Albarn" Hula Hoops advert. This was indeed sheer mass appeal.

● ● ●

The foreign dates for *The Great Escape* were lengthy and comprehensive. Starting with a few gigs in America, they moved on through Europe to Japan, then back to Britain for the Christmas shows, then Brazil for a one-off festival and finally back to America and Europe, finishing at Amsterdam's Paradiso Club on March 22, 1996. This policy paid rich dividends in Europe with *The Great Escape* being better received than any previous Blur album. Although there was

**Blur's front row bit of roughage**

as much difficulty relating to Blur's peculiar Englishness on the Continent as there was in America, they seemed more willing to try. In fact, sales were so high in southern Europe that each gig was sold out in advance.

The historically difficult American dates were marred right at the start when Damon was threatened at gun point. He and Alex were in a car heading for The Black Cat club in Washington DC when the singer gave the beady eye to a passing car. This was something he had always done – *Melody Maker* used to run a feature called "Each Week Damon From Blur Causes The Rest Of The Band To Have Seven Shades Of Shit Beaten Out Of Them." Unfortunately in America this isn't wise, and the car he stared at was crammed with fully armed home boys. One pulled his gun, pointed it at Damon's temple and said "Pow, pow", then the car screeched away. Later that night, four songs into the set, Damon introduced 'Top Man' and said: "This next song is about blokes who go out getting pissed and being naughty. Until four hours ago this seemed like a hard song, but now it seems soft."

The posters for this small tour announced "Be prepared for a shower of Evian" in the wake of Damon's previous Stateside troubles. Attendances were high, although the venues were small, and the crowds clearly knew the material well. The Internet was covered in gig reviews throughout this tour and the response was ecstatic, including one site which listed "Twenty Reasons Why Blur Are The Best Band Ever", including "they don't sing about walls, and they all have two eyebrows". Blur were now on Virgin Records (like SBK, a division of multi-national EMI) and although success was still limited, the band/record company relationship was much stronger.

Unfortunately, throughout the lengthy tour, the band suffered from a series of illnesses, which for a change were not abuse-related. Graham began to suffer from repetitive strain injury on his hands, a condition which had allegedly forced Elastica's bassist Annie Holland to quit her band completely. Dave contracted gastro-enteritis before the band's Belfast King's Hall show and was briefly hospitalised. At that evening's gig, Damon stepped on a piece of broken glass and lacerated his foot, causing him to attend the MTV award ceremony with a walking stick. Despite all these difficulties, no gigs were cancelled and Blur's excellent progress continued.

● ● ●

Blur's continued failure to crack the American market has been well documented, from the disastrous 44 date début tour to the most recent gun incident. It seems that success in the UK simply cannot easily be replicated across the Atlantic, and as far as Blur are concerned history is not in their favour.

America is the biggest rock market of them all, but until 1964 no British act had made any serious or lasting impression across the Atlantic. In that year everything changed for ever. The Beatles, fresh, exciting and quite unlike anything America had ever experienced before, took the country by storm leading what was known as

The British invasion, and since then there has been a steady parade of British bands who've made their fortunes in America. Generally speaking the groups most likely to succeed in the US are those whose music is based, albeit loosely, on blues and R&B. The Rolling Stones initiated the concept of selling 'old' black American music to 'young' white Americans and the tradition was continued with spectacular returns by The Who and Led Zeppelin in the seventies. In their wake, many British hard rock and heavy metal acts flourished in the US, from Black Sabbath and Deep Purple to Whitesnake, Def Leppard and more.

Certain British singer-songwriters, most notably Elton John, have also found huge fan bases in the States, but what Elton and the heavy brigade had in common – and The Police and U2 for that matter – was a willingness to tour unceasingly, to spend months on the road promoting their music. This, it is generally accepted, is essential if an act has serious designs on the almighty dollar.

Bands reluctant to tour regularly, especially those whose music relies on an English twist of the tongue, have found the US market more difficult to penetrate. Notable casualties over the years have been The Kinks (although their US plans were scuppered by a Union ban), T Rex, Slade, The Jam, Madness and, most recently, Suede. All have failed in a territory that represents 40% of the world's market, making it a costly frustration.

While American rock acts have little difficulty persuading us to enjoy romantic images of Americana, the reverse is seldom the case. Mention Primrose Hill or Camden Town and suddenly US interest dries up. Blur fit into this litany of great British bands who struggle in America, and are probably doomed to fail unless they change the underlying themes of their music. David Bowie won a small Stateside following for his gender bending, space age early material, but he didn't really cross over into the mainstream until his 1975 album *Young Americans*, a record based largely on soul and R&B.

British bands rarely tour hard enough – The Cranberries had to tour for 12 months before eventually cracking the market on a massive scale – and they are Irish. Bush, a British band who have enjoyed great Stateside success, actually based themselves over there for the same reason. PJ Harvey and Elastica have committed themselves to touring and reaped substantial benefits. On *The Great Escape* Blur toured three times, but each series of dates was only a month long.

Some British bands openly mock the country when they arrive. Suede infamously derided the States on their début tour there and were sent packing pretty quickly. They even had to change their name to The London Suede to avoid legal action from an MOR singer who called herself Suede. Brett's sexual dalliances and gender bending were just not acceptable to America – neither were Freddie Mercury's – and his apparent distaste for the US made this worse.

Damon frequently and aggressively suggested America

see this as tiresome whinging. Besides, in the early Eighties, when Eurythmics, The Human League and Culture Club dominated American airwaves and charts, native bands had experienced similar indifference. One frustrated Los Angeles band, X, even wrote a song about it, saying "Will the last American band to get played on the radio please bring the flag?"

Language problems sometimes arise. Slade's colloquialised titles like 'Mama Weer All Crazee Now' were hardly understood outside the Black Country, let alone 3,000 miles away. One of the more simple factors that contributed to the utter failure of *Modern Life* was the title. The word 'rubbish' is foreign to the American vocabulary, and this simple semantic clash is perhaps indicative of Blur's problems. *Modern Life Is Trash* just doesn't have the same echo.

Blur are not alone. While Britpop bands flew the flag at home, much of their parochial pop was ignored in America. Only Elastica and Oasis enjoyed any sizeable success, both through heavy touring, with the latter finally reaching the *Billboard* Top 5 in early 1996 with their second album. Meanwhile, Blur's chart topping *The Great Escape* barely dented the *Billboard* Top 200 and disappeared after only one week. *Modern Life* was so unsuccessful (a paltry 33,000 sales) that most Blur fans over there haven't even heard of it. *Leisure* sold more than *Parklife*, and neither topped 100,000. Damon's statement that "The only thing we have in common with Oasis is that we are both doing shit in America" is now woefully inaccurate.

Oasis, with their wall of guitars sound and introspective, non-specific lyrics, are catering to American tastes. Quirky English pop tunes do not fit easily into the AOR rock radio programming which dictates much of what succeeds there. One source at Virgin Records claims that

a memo had been circulated to all independent radio pluggers early in 1996 to completely forget Blur and concentrate on Oasis, even going so far as to suggest that this was because Blur might not be around much longer. Older Brits such as Rod Stewart, Phil Collins and Eric Clapton enjoy success largely because their more recent music 'sounds American'. The best selling CD in the USA in 1994 was Ace Of Base, so a parky singing about pigeons shagging has hardly got much chance.

There were some positive signs on the second American leg of the *Great Escape* dates in January and February 1996. Although record sales were still very low, attendances at live shows were disproportionately high, with venues of 2,000-3,000 selling out well in advance. Also, some of their gigs were broadcast live on radio in various States. Damon was more realistic this time around when he told *Melody Maker*: "America feels good this time around, but only time will tell if it's a fad or something that's gonna make sense to people there." He wasn't about to give in either, as he told *Melody Maker*: "We don't like chickening out of something. It's a challenge. It vaguely annoys me when people say we've never done anything in America – we went four months touring there with *Leisure*. We've gone there every year, we sell out 3,000 venues across the country and songs like 'Girls & Boys' go Top 50." Also, in April 1996, they were booked to play at the opening of the New York Virgin Megastore, the world's biggest record shop, and Damon was quick to point out that their venues were the same size as those played by Radiohead, a band widely hailed as a recent US success.

Nevertheless, it remains an uphill struggle for Blur. Mike Shea, publisher of *Alternative Press*, the most respected alternative magazine in America is quite clear about Blur's failure to translate in his home country: "'Girls & Boys' did well in the clubs but was seen over here as a novelty song, and people just never got the whole English Sixties/Kinks background. Blur's style doesn't work over here – the catchy, cute, accessible music and English themes just aren't universally accepted. Even though Blur were here first, it appears that Oasis have cracked America and that Blur probably never will. In the midst of all The Beatles re-issues, the mainstream rock'n'roll fans in the US have bought into Oasis, their sulking, pouting rock is infinitely more palatable to Americans. People will take Oasis as the only Brit band, but that's it, they don't want any more. If you turn on any alternative commercial radio in 1996 you will hear Oasis 40 times a week minimum and you'll be lucky to get Blur ten times."

This sense of frustration in America added to a growing, nagging feeling that all was not well in the Blur camp. This was compounded by Oasis' success both there and at home. Since the 'Battle Of Britain' and Noel's Aids comment, Oasis have leapt ahead. Their second album *(What's The Story) Morning Glory?* was tepidly received by the critics but paradoxically loved by the public. It sold 350,000 in its first week alone, the biggest sales since Michael Jackson's *Bad* and was the No. 1 album in Britain for months. After a slow start, the Gallagher Brothers became the pop world's lippiest dollar millionaires. A trio of Brit awards and two nights at Earl's Court, the country's biggest indoor gig, confirmed that Oasis was now the biggest band in the country, despite all their personnel problems. It was an astonishing triumph.

Blur meanwhile were plagued by press rumours of a split, with many fingers pointing at Alex's growing distance from the other members of the band. He still loved the pop star life, the Groucho Club, the champagne and the fame, and there were media intimations of escalating drug use. Alex himself bragged that he drank for six days solidly then had one day off to clean up. Graham told *NME* that he resented this: "I hate a lot of the things that Alex stands for. I don't want people to think it's what this band is about. All that Groucho Club bollocks and him going on about birds and boozing all the time, I hate that."

Graham has come to blows with Alex over this. He told one magazine the factors he thought might split the band would be "death, or if we made another *Parklife*. I don't think we could carry on if one of us left... unless it was Alex." Graham also tired of the way people always assumed Damon's views were his when he told *NME*: "If he goes on about football and page three girls that means we all get associated with it. I hate football and hate page three girls, but people always want to hear Damon's opinion."

With Graham unfairly tagged as 'the unofficial strangest man in pop', his thoughts were open to intrusive media speculation, and his drinking habits were often mentioned. When one journalist approached him during a quiet pint and said "Aren't you Graham out of Blur?" he answered "Only when I'm working." There were suggestions that Damon and Alex were also at loggerheads, and that Alex felt the singer and guitarist were siding against him.

For his part, Damon said he was tired of the excesses of some of his friends, telling *Q* magazine: "There's a blizzard of cocaine and I hate it." Some even suggested that Dave was tiring of the lifestyle and, being well into his thirties, was finding it increasingly difficult to leave his family for each tour.

Others worried about the dilemma that Blur's massive success had created – with huge status in the UK and great success in Europe, what aspirations would Blur be left with if America continued to close its doors? Would they risk self-parody consolidating their successful territories or alternatively release increasingly obscure music and plummet in popularity? Also, *The Great Escape* had sold well initially in the UK, but its chart life had not nearly matched *Parklife* and in a world where constant commercial improvement is vital, questions were asked. Despite exceptional reviews in the press, including becoming only the second band to win two *Q* Album Of The Year Awards, the general feeling was that *The Great Escape* had slowed down Blur's success somewhat. This fuelled the split theories still more.

Spring of 1996 was full of such rumours, none of them remotely substantiated. Matters were not helped with several churlish television appearances, including an appearance on Chris Evans' *TFI Friday* when Damon seemed bitter about their lack of success at The Brits and made derisory side remarks about Alex. For one prime-time Italian TV show Alex missed the plane and Graham was officially excused from performing as he was moving house. Graham was replaced with a cardboard cut-out, and Smoggy, Blur's head of security, shouldered Alex's bass. Needless to say, this emerged in the press as Blur on the verge of falling apart.

Smoggy on bass
after Alex missed his plane

If Blur do split, their achievements in British music should be acknowledged and the band allowed to announce their decision with dignity and in their own time. It would be a shock, since their resolve has always been impressive, as Graham said to *Melody Maker*: "I don't think there has ever been a time when we felt like giving up. Even during the dark years, we had this feeling it would all come right in the end." He also doubted that they would stand alone musically, as he told *NME*: "We can make good music together but God

knows what might happen if we tried to make music individually, it'd be shit."

It is to be hoped that the rumours are unfounded, because apart from their importance to British music, Blur are in a stronger position now than they have *ever* been. Firstly, *The Great Escape* is actually a *bigger* commercial success than its more famed predecessor *Parklife*. By March of 1996, *The Great Escape* had already overtaken *Parklife's* world-wide sales figures of 1.8 million, and by the start of April, the fourth album had passed the two million mark. This time around, Blur have cleaned up in Europe, an equivalent sized territory to the USA. Whereas they were being asked to play on European festival bills, now they are being asked to headline. Their 1996 schedule is already booked with huge open air shows of their own at the 38,000 seat Dublin RDS in June as well as massive festival headline slots all over the Continent. Their regular tour dates are usually 3-4,000 each night, with 9,000 not uncommon. In Spain alone, their sales have increased from 20,000 for *Parklife* to 80,000 for *The Great Escape*. This fourth album has, despite all assumptions otherwise, far outstripped *Parklife* commercially.

Secondly, *The Great Escape* was also an album of crucial importance musically. It has cleared the debris of preconceptions that were threatening to suffocate Blur's creativity. The musical complexity and more sombre tone has already prepared listeners for something much darker, harsher and probably far less commercial. It was their own musical great escape to release the record when they did.

Thirdly, the fact that Oasis have stolen the commercial limelight is actually a hidden blessing – now the spotlight is off Blur, leaving them free to pursue whatever musical goals they wish, free from narrow public expectations. They cannot afford to release many more narrative tales about sexual deviants in London's suburbia. Damon has already made overtones towards a more personal, yet more universal style of writing: "I can sit at my piano and write brilliant observational English pop songs all day, but you've got to move on." Damon is listening to jungle, African music and has expressed a keen interested in writing a musical. Graham is absorbed in obscure US underground bands and has learnt to play the banjo. Being perceived as underdogs, despite *The Great Escape's* massive success, has given Blur this freedom.

Fourthly, comparisons with the Mancunian band are unjustified. Suggesting Blur have failed because Oasis have succeeded is like suggesting the Stones failed because The Beatles sold more records. Oasis and Blur are at opposite ends of the musical spectrum. The criteria by which to judge a band's success should be their own musical creativity and their continued commercial progress relative to their previous work. On both counts *The Great Escape* was Blur's most successful project to date.

Finally, Blur are ready and prepared to make a change. After the February 1996 release of the No. 7 single 'Stereotypes', Damon was already making it clear that they were looking towards wildly different musical pastures from previous work. In an article in *The Big Issue*, Damon started by announcing that Britpop was dead: "Britpop as an idea is no longer valid, it's no longer challenging." Elsewhere he told *NME*: "It's all over now. We killed Britpop, we chopped it up and put it under the patio long ago. And any band which is still Britpop in a year's time is in serious trouble." He was so keen to distance himself from the movement that he appeared almost desperate: "I didn't call it Britpop and I never will. We didn't invent anything – we just made British-sounding music sell a lot of records."

Blur realise they have to change now or they, like their peers, will risk self-parody. Graham was ahead of even this – during the recording of *The Great Escape* all he listened to was obscure American hardcore. "I don't know anyone from the groups that astound me or inspire me because they are all American," he said. The tide is turning – in March 1996, Compulsion released an anti-Britpop single entitled 'Question Time For The Proles' which they said was "a backlash against Britpop and its misplaced nostalgia."

Maybe 'Country House' and the Battle of Britain killed Britpop. Maybe it was Mile End, an unbeatable peak. Already there is a terrace element that remember 'Parklife' as a yob sing-along, and there are parts of *Parklife* that have been lost to crass commercialist culture – in twenty years time, it will be sad if all Blur are remembered for is the thuggish chant of "Parklife". Musically, it may well be that *The Great Escape is* hailed as a 'hidden' treasure, just as The Kinks' *The Village Green Preservation Society* assumed greater importance once the band were allowed the luxury of hindsight. In order to maintain the degree of integrity and uniqueness they have mustered so far, Blur must once again change. They can do it, because they have done so in the past with greater success than any of their contemporaries.

The next single 'Charmless Man' scheduled for release in April 1996, may well be the end of an era but the start of a new phase. Within a week of returning from their lengthy world tour, Damon had flown out to Iceland to continue writing the new album, working on demos that had been started on the previous winter's arena tour. There are rumours of possibly two albums, one with hard guitar and the other a mellower collection. There are talks of six months or more in the studio, away from the album-tour-album-tour treadmill they have been on for the last two years. Even solo work has been discussed.

In the spring of 1996, Damon was talking up the forthcoming changes still more: "All I've got are just songs on a Walkman, but we want to have a bit more anarchy in the way we record. Having worked with someone like Tricky, who goes in the studio and has no regard for convention at all and does things you shouldn't that sound great, that was quite a revelation to me. I'd like to work more with that sort of attitude." The relationship with Stephen Street is already pencilled in to continue, and the band are planning to start recording in the spring and summer. Yet another autumn album is not impossible, although the commercial success of *The Great Escape* has been so widespread in Europe that they are already contemplating delaying the new material until that fourth album has finally slowed down.

● ● ●

Blur are an exceptional band on many levels. With such a vast cannon of popular music preceding them, they have plundered the past to create something for the future, and in the process they have inspired a generation that once again celebrates British music. Damon is by any standards an exceptional talent. His star quality has always been evident, but it is his ability to amalgamate his many artistic, musical, theatrical and cultural influences that marks him as particularly gifted. His contributions to Blur swing from theatrical to punk, middle class to working class, art school to football terrace, and from the East End to the Far East – everything he writes and delivers is a great melting pot of diversity. In many senses, he cannot be adequately quantified.

Few contemporaries have developed this much as a band over four albums – they are critically acclaimed millionaires and stars of all corners of the media, and yet their début album sounds like another band. Blur have killed several musical movements and created a few along the way. They have brought humour, musical excellence, great live shows and thematical brilliance to a British music scene littered with banality. In so doing, they have already made an indelible mark on music history. With so many achievements behind them, Blur's goals for the future have inevitably changed, and Damon is understandably excited about the band's potential that has only just begun to blossom: "I no longer care about being famous. I don't have to look to chart positions anymore. We don't need to be the biggest band on the planet anymore, just the best."

Graham has been known to collapse on stage

# Discography

# Singles

**She's So High (Edit)/I Know**
Food FOOD 26 (7")
**November 1990**

**She's So High (Definitive)/
I Know (Extended)**
Food 12BLURIAA (12" Promo Only)
**November 1990**

**She's So High (Definitive)/Sing/
I Know**
Food 12FOOD (12")
**November 1990**

**She's So High (Edit)/I Know**
Food TCFOOD 26 (Cassette)
**November 1990**

**She's So High/
I Know (Extended)/Down**
Food CDFOOD 26 (CD)
**November 1990**

**There's No Other Way/Inertia**
Food FOOD 29 (7")
**March 1991**

**There's No Other Way
(Extended)/Inertia/Mr Briggs/
I'm All Over**
Food 12FOOD 29 (12")
**March 1991**

**There's No Other Way
(The Blur Remix)/Won't Do It/
Day Upon Day (Live)**
Food 12FOODX 29 (12")
**March 1991**

**There's No Other Way
(Extended)/There's No Other
Way (The Blur Remix)**
Food 12FOODDJ 29 (12")
**March 1991**

**There's No Other Way/Inertia**
Food TCFOOD 29 (Cassette)
**March 1991**

**There's No Other Way/Inertia/
Mr Briggs/I'm All Over**
Food CDFOOD 29 (CD)
**March 1991**

**Bang/Luminous**
Food FOOD 31 (7")
**July 1991**

**Bang (Extended)/Explain/
Luminous/Uncle Love**
Food 12FOOD 31 (12")
**July 1991**

**Bang (Edit)/Bang (Unedited)**
Food 12FOOD DJ31 (12")
**July 1991**

**Bang/Luminous**
Food TCFOOD 31 (Cassette)
**July 1991**

**Bang/Explain/Luminous/Berserk**
Food CDFOOD 31 (CD)
**July 1991**

**Popscene/Mace**
Food FOOD 37 (7")
**March 1992**

**Popscene (Edit)/
Popscene (Unedited)**
Food BLURDJ 37 (12")
**March 1992**

**Popscene**
Food 12BLUR 5 (12" One-sided Promo Only)
**March 1992**

**Popscene/I'm Fine/Mace/
Garden Central**
Food 12FOOD 37 (12")
**March 1992**

**Popscene/Mace**
Food TCFOOD 37 (Cassette)
**March 1992**

**Popscene/Mace/Badgeman Brown**
Food CDFOOD 37 (CD)
**March 1992**

**Popscene (Edit)/Popscene**
Food CDBLURDJ 37 (CD)
**March 1992**

**For Tomorrow/Into Another/
Hanging Over**
Food TCFOOD 40 (Cassette)
**April 1993**

**For Tomorrow (Visit To
Primrose Hill Extended)/
Into Another/ Hanging Over**
Food 12FOODDJ 40 (12")
**April 1993**

**For Tomorrow/Into Another/
Hanging Over/Peach**
Food 12FOOD 40 (12")
**April 1993**

**For Tomorrow (Visit To
Primrose Hill Extended)/
Peach/Bone Bag**
Food CDFOOD 40 (CD)
**April 1993**

**For Tomorrow (Single Version)/
When The Cows Come Home/
Beachcoma/For Tomorrow
(Acoustic Version)**
Food CDSFOOD 40 (CD)
**April 1993**

**Chemical World/Maggie May**
Food FOOD 45 (7" Red Vinyl)
**June 1993**

**Chemical World/Es Smecht/
Young And Lively/My Ark**
Food 12FOOD 45 (12" with print)
**June 1993**

**Chemical World/Young And
Lively/Es Smecht/My Ark**
Food CDSFOOD 45 (CD)
**June 1993**

**Chemical World/
Never Clever (Live)/
Pressure On Julian (Live)/
Come Together (Live)**
Food CDFOODS 45 (CD)
**June 1993**

**Chemical World (Single Edit)/
Chemical World (Reworked)**
Food CDFOODDJ 45 (CD)
**June 1993**

**Sunday Sunday/Tell Me Tell Me**
Food FOODS 46 (7" Yellow Vinyl)
**October 1993**

**Sunday Sunday/Long Legged/
Mixed Up**
Food 12FOODS 46 (12")
**October 1993**

**Sunday Sunday/Dizzy/Fried/
Shimmer**
Food CDFOODS 46 (CD)
**October 1993**

**The Sunday Sunday
Popular Community Song CD:
Sunday Sunday/Daisy Bell/
Let's All Go Down The Strand**
Food CDFOODX 46 (CD)
**October 1993**

**Girls & Boys/Magpie/
People In Europe**
Food FOODS 47 (7")
**March 1994**

**Girls & Boys**
Food 12FOODDJ 47
(12" One-sided Promo Only)
**March 1994**

**Girls & Boys (Pet Shop
Boys 12" Remix)/Girls & Boys
(Pet Shop Boys 7" Remix)**
Food 12FOODGB 47 (12")
**March 1994**

**Girls & Boys/Magpie/
People In Europe**
Food TCFOOD 47 (Cassette)
**March 1994**

**Girls & Boys/Magpie/
Anniversary Waltz**
Food CDFOODS 47 (CD)
**March 1994**

**Girls & Boys/People In
Europe/ Peter Panic**
Food CDFOODX 47 (CD)
**March 1994**

**Girls & Boys/
Girls & Boys (Pet Shop Boys
7" Remix)/Girls & Boys
(Pet Shop Boys 12" Remix)**
Food CDFOODDJ 47 (CD)
**March 1994**

**Girls & Boys (Pet Shop Boys
7" Remix)/Girls & Boys
(Pet Shop Boys 12" Remix)**
Food CDFOODGB 47 (CD)
**March 1994**

**To The End/Girls & Boys
(Pet Shop Boys 7" Remix)/
Girls & Boys (Pet Shop Boys
12" Remix)**
Food 12FOOD 50 (12")
**May 1994**

**To The End/Girls & Boys
(Pet Shop Boys 7" Remix)/
Girls & Boys (Pet Shop Boys
12" Remix)**
Food 12FOOD 50 (12" Die Cut Sleeve)
**May 1994**

**To The End/Girls & Boys
(Pet Shop Boys 7" Remix)/
Threadneedle Street**
Food TCFOOD 50 (Cassette)
**May 1994**

**To The End/Threadneedle
Street/ Got Yer!**
Food CDFOODS 50 (CD)
**May 1994**

**To The End/Girls & Boys
(Pet Shop Boys 7" Remix)/
Girls & Boys (Pet Shop Boys
12" Remix)**
Food CDFOOD 50 (CD)
**May 1994**

**Parklife/Supa Shoppa**
Food FOOD LH 53 (7")
**September 1994**

**Parklife/Supa Shoppa/
To The End (French Version)/
Beard**
Food 12FOOD 53 (12")
**September 1994**

**Parklife/Supa Shoppa/To The End
(with Françoise Hardy)/Beard**
Food TCFOOD 53 (Cassette)
**September 1994**

**Parklife/Beard/
To The End (French Version)**
Food CDFOOD 53 (CD)
**September 1994**

**Parklife/Supa Shoppa/
Theme From An Imaginary Film**
Food CDFOODS 53 (CD)/
Food CDFOODDJ 53 (Promo CD)
**September 1994**

**End Of A Century/Red Necks**
Food FOODS56 (7")/
Food TCFOOD 56 (Cassette)
**November 1994**

**End Of A Century/Red Necks/
Alex's Song**
Food CDFOOD 56 (CD)
**November 1994**

**End Of A Century**
Food CDFOOD DJ 56 (Promo CD)
**November 1994**

**Country House/
One Born Every Minute**
Food FOOD 63 (7")/
Food TCFOOD 63 (Cassette)
**August 1995**

Country House/
One Born Every Minute/
To The End (French Version)
Food CDFOOD 63 (CD)
August 1995

Country House (Live From
Mile End)/Girls & Boys (Live
From Mile End)/Parklife (Live
From Mile End)/For Tomorrow
(Live From Mile End)
Food CDFOODS 63 (Limited Edition CD)
August 1995

Country House
EMI 12FOODDJ 63 (CD Promo)
August 1995

The Universal
EMI 12FOODDJ 68
(12" Promo 1045 copies Only)
November 1995

The Universal/Entertain Me
(The Live It! Remix)
Food TCFOOD 69 (Cassette)
November 1995

The Universal/Ultranol/
No Monsters In Me/Entertain Me
(The Live It! Remix)
Food FOODS 69 (CD)
November 1995

The Universal/
Mr Robinson's Quango/
It Could Be You/Stereotypes
(All Tracks Recorded Live
At Beeb)
Food FOOD 69 (CD) (Live At The Beeb)
November 1995

Stereotypes/
The Man Who Left Himself/Tame
Food FOOD 73 (7")/
Food TCFOOD 73 (Cassette)
February 1996

Stereotypes/
The Man Who Left Himself/
Tame/Ludwig
Food CDFOOD 73 (CD)
February 1996

Charmless Man/The Horrors
Food FOOD 76 (7")/
Food TCFOOD 76 (Cassette)
April 1996

Charmless Man/The Horrors/
A Song/St. Louis
Food CDFOOD 76 (CD)
April 1996

# Albums

### LEISURE
She's So High/Bang/Slow Down/
Repetition/Bad Day/Sing/
There's No Other Way/Fool/
Come Together/High Cool/
Birthday/Wear Me Down
Food FOODLP 6/Food FOODCD 6/
FOODTC 6
August 1991

### MODERN LIFE IS RUBBISH
For Tomorrow/Advert/Colin Zeal/
Pressure On Julian/Star Shaped/
Blue Jeans/Chemical World/
Sunday Sunday/Oily Water/
Miss America/Villa Rosie/Coping/
Turn It Up/Resigned
Food FOODLP 9/Food FOODCD 9/
Food FOODTC 9
May 1993

### PARKLIFE
Girls & Boys/Tracy Jacks/
End Of A Century/Parklife/
Bank Holiday/Badhead/
The Debt Collector/Far Out/
To The End/London Loves/
Trouble In The Message Centre/
Clover Over Dover/
Magic America/Jubilee/
This Is A Low/Lot 105
Food FOODLP 10/Food FOODCD 10/
Food FOODTC 10/
(Japanese Edition has greyhounds
lighting up and braking on opening)
April 1994

### THE GREAT ESCAPE
Stereotypes/Country House/
Best Days/Charmless Man/
Fade Away/Top Man/
The Universal/Mr Robinson's
Quango/He Thought Of Cars/
It Could Be You/Ernold Same/
Globe Alone/Dan Abnormal/
Entertain Me/Yuko And Hiro
Food FOODCD 14/Food FOODLP 14/
Food FOODTC 14
September 1995

### BLUR PRESENT THE SPECIAL
### COLLECTORS EDITION
Day Upon Day (Live)/Inertia/
Luminous/Mace/Badgeman
Brown/Hanging Over/Peach/
When The Cows Come Home/
Maggie May/Es Smecht/Fried
(Blur featuring Seymour)/
Anniversary Waltz/Threadneedle
Street/Got Yer!/Supa Shoppa/
Beard/Theme From An Imaginary
Film/Bank Holiday
Food TOCP 8395 (CD)
(Japanese import only)
1995

### JAPANESE LIVE ALBUM -
Title to be announced
Recorded live at Budokan in
November 1995 Scheduled
release date summer 1996

# Videos

### STAR SHAPED
Promos and footage of tours
from mid-1991 to mid-1993:
Intermission/Explain/
There's No Other Way/

Luminous/She's So High (Edit)/
Colin Zeal/Popscene/
When Will We Be Married/
Sunday Sunday/Wassailing Song/
Coping
PMI (EMI) MVP 4911453
September 1993

### STAR SHAPED
Promos only PMI EMI MVL 4914013
February 1995

### SHOWTIME
Blur Live at Alexandra Palace,
October 1995
Lot 105/Sunday Sunday/Jubilee/
Tracy Jacks/Magic America/
End Of A Century/Popscene/
Trouble In The Message Centre/
She's So High/Chemical World/
Badhead/There's No Other Way
PMI (EMI) MVN 4914023
February 1995

Out Of My Head: Girls And Boys
Astrion Plc AST 1012
(Various Artists compilation)
June 1995

# Miscellaneous

Various Book Club
Special editions of some of
the following are available by
Britannia Music – same
catalogue numbers apply, with
a 'BM' prefix

The Incredible Sound
Machine: Down
Parlophone CDISM 1 (CD Promo Only)
December 1990

The Parlophone Select Tape:
Come Together
Parlophone TCSELECT 1
(Various Artists compilation Cassette Only
Given Away Free With Select)
April 1991

Forever Changing:
I Know (Extended)
Beechwood Music EVER 001CD (CD)/
EVER 001MC (Cassette)/EVER 001LP (LP)
(Various Artists compilation)
August 1991

Awesome!! 2:
There's No Other Way
EMI CDEVP 1 (CD)/ TCEVP 1(Cassette)/
EVP 1 (LP) (Various Artists compilation)
October 1991

Volume Two: Oily Water
Volume (Worlds End) V2CD
(Various Artists compilation CD)
November 1991

High Cool (Easy Listening Mix)/
Bad Day (Remix)
Food 12BLUR 4 (12" 1,000 only Promo)
November 1991

Food Christmas Party:
Resigned (Demo)/
High Cool (Easy Listening Mix)
Food TCFOOD 34 (Cassette Only)
(Various Artists Compilation, given away
free at Food's 1991 Christmas Party)

Precious: There's No Other Way
Dino Entertainment DINMC 38 (Cassette)/
DINTV3 8 (10" LP)
(Various Artists compilation)
June 1992

Reading: The Indie Album:
There's No Other Way
Polygram 5156482 (CD)/5156481 (LP)
(Various Artists compilation CD)
September 1992

In A Field Of Their Own -
Glastonbury '92:
Sunday Sunday (Live)
NME GLASTON1 DCD
(Various Artists compilation CD)
September 1992

Ruby Trax -
The NME's Roaring Forty:
Maggie May
NME 40 CD (Various Artists Compilation CD)
October 1992

The Wassailing Song
Food BLUR 6 (7")
Given away free at
1992 Christmas show

Star Shaped/Sunday Sunday/
Advert/For Tomorrow/Resigned
Food CD5-CDMLIR1
(CD Sampler for Modern Life Is Rubbish)
May 1993

Peace Together: Oliver's Army
Island CID 8018/ILPS8018 (LP)/
ICT8018 (Cassette)
(Various Artists compilation)
June 1993

Great Expectations:
For Tomorrow (Live)
XFM CD1 (Various Artists compilation CD)
July 1993

**Who Covers Who: Substitute**
CM Discs CM 006CD (CD)/CM 006 (LP)
(Various Artists compilation of
The Who Covers)
August 1993

**Wasted 1: Sunday Sunday/Advert**
EMI CDWASTED1 (CD)/WASTED1
(Cassette)
August 1993

**Five Alive Take 2: Advert**
**(Mark Goodier Session Version)**
MMMC 2 (Cassette Only)
Melody Maker Various Artists compilation,
given away free
October 1993

**Indie Top 20 No.8:**
**Chemical World**
Beechwood Music TT018MC (Cassette)/
TT018LP (LP) (Various Artists compilation)
November 1993

**Bet Bet Bet**
**(4 track sampler for Parklife)**
Food FOODCD 5
April 1994

**Tip Sheet CD 52: To The End**
Tip Sheet TIPSHEET 52
(Various Artists compilation CD)
May 1994

**Indie Top 20: Sunday Sunday**
Beechwood Music TT019CD (CD)/
TT019MC (Cassette)
(Various Artists compilation Double Album)
May 1994

**Sure Shot: End Of A Century**
Parlophone (EMI) SURECD1 (Various Artists
compilation CD)
August 1994

**Now That's What I Call Music**
**No 28: Girls And Boys**
EMI/Virgin/Polygram CDNOW 28 (CD)/
TCNOW 28 (Cassette)/NOW 28 (LP)
(Various Artists compilation)
August 1994

**1994 Mercury Music Prize**
**Sampler: Tracy Jacks**
Mercury Music MMPCD 3 (CD)/
MMPTC 3 (Cassette) (Promo Sampler
for 1994 Mercury Music Awards)
August 1994

**Club Together: Girls And Boys**
**(Pet Shop Boys 12" Remix)**
EMI CDEMC 3692 (CD)/TCEMC 3692
(Cassette)/EMC 3692 (LP)
(Various Artists compilation Double Album)
September 1994

**Now That's What I Call Music**
**1994: Girls And Boys**
EMI/Virgin/Polygram CDNOW1994
(CD)/TCNOW1994 (Cassette)
(Various Artists compilation Double Album)
September 1994

**Now That's What I Call Music**
**No.29: Parklife**
EMI/Virgin/Polygram CDNOW29 (CD)/
TCNOW29 (Cassette)/NOW29 (LP)
(Various Artists compilation Double Album)
October 1994

**Vox: Class Of '94:**
**He Thought Of Cars**
VOXGIVIT 14 (Cassette)
(Various Artists compilation, given away
free with Vox magazine)
November 1994

**NME Brat Pack '95: This Is A Low**
NMEBRAT 95 (Various Artists compilation,
given away free with NME)
January 1995

**Tip Sheet CD 92: For Tomorrow**
Tip Sheet TIPSHEET 92
(Various Artists compilation CD)
February 1995

**Unlaced: Girls And Boys**
EMI CDEMTV 90/TCEMTV 90 (Cassette)
(Various Artists compilation)
February 1995

**NME Singles Of The Week 1994:**
**Girls And Boys (Edit)**
NMERCACD3 (CD)
(Various Artists compilation, given away
free with NME)
March 1995

**Q/EMI CD: This Is A Low**
(CD) (Various Artists compilation Given
Away Free With Q)
April 1995

**Shine: Twenty Brilliant Indie**
**Hits: Parklife**
Polygram 5255672 (CD)/525567 (LP)
(Various Artists compilation)
May 1995

**Tempus Fugit (Alex James)**
**B Side to Duffy single**
**'Sugar High b/w Tempus Fugit/**
**Vision Of Bliss/**
**The Sugar On The Pill**
Indolent (BMG) DUFF 002CD (CD Single)
July 199

**Drive: She's So High**
October 95 (Various Artists compilation
Cassette Only Given Away Free With Q)
September 1995

**Get Real! Holsten Indie Party:**
**To The End**
EMI BMCDGET 01 (CD)/
BMTCGet 01 (Cassette)/BMGET 01 (LP)
September 1995

**Help: Eine Kleine Lift Muzak**
Go! Discs CD: 828682/2 Cassette: 828682/
4 LP: 828682/1 (Various Artists compilation)
October 1995

**Now That's What I Call Music**
**1995: Country House**
EMI/Virgin/Polygram CDNOW1995 (CD)/
TCNOW1995 (Cassette)/NOW1995 (LP)
(Various Artists compilation Double Album)
October 1995

**Parlophone Conference Sampler:**
**Charmless Man**
EMI VERY3 (CD) (Sampler Promo Only)
October 1995

**Our Price In-Store:**
**The Universal/Charmless Man**
Our Price INDEX 187 (CD Only)
October 1995

**Now That's What I Call Music**
**No.32: Country House**
EMI/Virgin/Polygram CDNOW32 (CD)/
TCNOW32 (Cassette)/NOW32 (LP)
(Various Artists compilation Double Album)
November 1995

**DMC 152/3/4: Girls And Boys**
152/3/4 (CD 850 copies Promo Only)/
DMC 152/3/4
(Cassette 1300 copies Promo Only)
November 1995

**Shine No.3: End Of A Century**
Polygram 5259652 (CD)/5259653 (Cassette)/
5259654 (LP) (Various Artists compilation)
November 1995

**Mastermix: Classix Cuts:**
**There's No Other Way**
Megabass CC14 (CD Only)
(Various Artists compilation)
December 1995

**NME Brat Pack '96: Top Man**
NMEBRAT 96 (Various Artists compilation,
given away free with NME)
January 1996

**The Best Album In The**
**World... Ever! Part 2: Parklife**
Virgin VTDCD 76 (CD)/
VTDMC 76 (Cassette)
(Various Artists compilation)
January 1996

**MTV Fresh: To The End**
MTV CDEMTV 111 (CD)/
TCEMTV 111 (Cassette)
(Various Artists compilation)
February 1996

**Live + Kickin': Girls And Boys**
MCA MCD60007 (CD)/MC60007 (Cassette)
(Various Artists compilation)
February 1996

**The Best Album In The**
**World... Ever!: Girls And Boys**
Virgin VTDCD 58 (CD)/
VTDMC 58 (Cassette)
(Various Artists compilation)
February 1996

**Trainspotting: Sing**
Premier (EMI) CDEMC 3739 (CD)/
TCEMC 3739 (Cassette)/EMC 3739 (LP)
(Various Artists compilation)
February 1996

**The Brit Awards: The Universal**
Sony SONYTV 10CD (CD)/
SONYTV 10MC (Cassette)(Various Artists
compilation From Brit Awards)
February 1996

**Now That's What I Call Music**
**No.33: The Universal**
EMI/Virgin/Polygram CDNOW33 (CD)/
TCNOW33 (Cassette)/NOW33 (LP)
(Various Artists compilation Double Album)
March 1996

**The Best Album Of The 90's**
**So Far: Parklife**
EMI CDEMTVD 116 (CD)/
TCEMTVD 116 (Cassette)
(Various Artists compilation)
March 1996

# American Promos

**Blur To Go (Four Live Tracks/**
**Bang (Remixed)**
DPRO 05455

**Basically Blur (Interview and**
**three acoustic tracks)**
Catalogue No. Unknown

**Focusing With Blur**
**(Interview and tracks)**
DPRO SBK 05424

# Laser Discs

**Pioneer 56 - UK Update:**
**Popscene**
Diamond Time 0692A
April 1992

**Disceyes: Sunday Sunday**
Diamond Time 1193P
October 1993

**Disceyes: Girls And Boys**
Diamond Time 0594G
March 1994

**Pioneer UK Natdisc:**
**Girls And Boys**
Diamond Time 0594I
May 1994

**VJB UK 159: Girls And Boys**
Diamond Time 0594F
May 1994

**VJB Euro 116: Girls And Boys**
Diamond Time 0694E
May 1994

**VJB German 116: Girls And Boys**
Diamond Time 0694D
May 1994

**VJBUK 162: To The End**
Diamond Time 0794/F
June 1994

**Tobysound: Chart Hit 162:**
**To The End**
Diamond Time 0894/V
June 1994

**VJB French 40: Girls And Boys**
Diamond Time 0894/K
July 1994

**Hankin: Girls And Boys**
Diamond Time 0894V
August 1994

**Pioneer French Natdisc:**
**Girls And Boys**
Diamond Time 0894J
September 1994

**Pioneer UK Natdisc 81:**
**To The End**
Diamond Time 0994/A
September 1994

**Pioneer UK Natdisc 87/2:**
**End Of A Century**
Diamond Time 0295/F
November 1994

**VJBUK No.168: End Of A Century**
Diamond Time 0295P
March 1995

**VJBUK No.173: She's So High**
Diamond Time 0895/1
April 1995

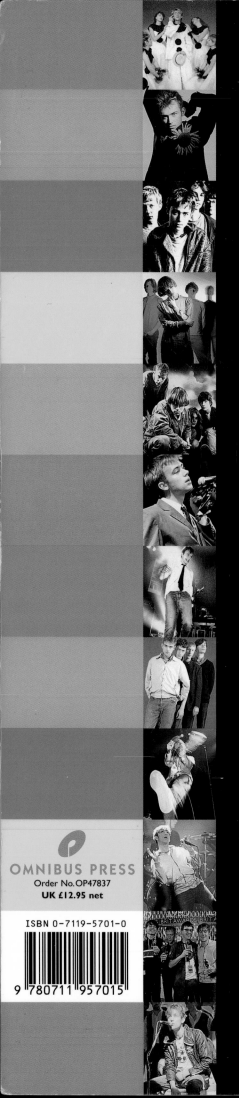

**blur** **The whole story** is the first full-length illustrated biography of Blur, whose vision of England in the Nineties — typified by the brilliant 'Parklife' album — has re-energised British pop music.

It follows the Blur story in consummate detail from their schooldays in and around Colchester, through early bands and Blur's formation, to the success of their most recent album 'The Great Escape'.

Led by the charming arrogance of blue-eyed pin-up Damon Albarn, Blur have accumulated plenty of Brits Awards, but it wasn't easy. Along the way they suffered brickbats from the media, drank themselves silly and occasionally hated each other...

*Blur: The whole story contains revealing information about...*

- *The lives of all four members before the band's formation...*
- *The struggles of their early incarnations before coming together as Blur and signing their first record deal...*
- *Fascinating insights into the personal and musical dilemmas the band have faced during their career, and the inspiration behind the decisions that have kept them on the road to success...*
- *Full details of their rivalry with Oasis, and why their place in musical history is assured regardless of the Mancunians' success...*

Author *Martin Roach* has interviewed several key figures in Blur's story to present the definitive biography of the definitive British band of the Nineties.

*Packed with scores of black & white and colour photographs, and including the most comprehensive Blur discography ever compiled.*

OMNIBUS PRESS
Order No. OP47837
UK £12.95 net

ISBN 0-7119-5701-0

9 780711 957015